CW00821690

# MURDER & CRIME

# ISLINGTON

# MURDER & CRIME

# ISLINGTON

## Peter Stubley

The History Press

First published 2012

The History Press
The Mill, Brimscombe Port
Stroud, Gloucestershire, GL5 2QG
www.thehistorypress.co.uk

© Peter Stubley 2012

The right of Peter Stubley to be identified as the Author
of this work has been asserted in accordance with the
Copyrights, Designs and Patents Act 1988.

All rights reserved. No part of this book may be reprinted
or reproduced or utilised in any form or by any electronic,
mechanical or other means, now known or hereafter invented,
including photocopying and recording, or in any information
storage or retrieval system, without the permission in writing
from the Publishers.
British Library Cataloguing in Publication Data.
A catalogue record for this book is available from the British Library.

ISBN 978 0 7524 6557 9

Typesetting and origination by The History Press
Printed in Great Britain

# CONTENTS

# Introduction

This book attempts to illustrate the history of Islington between the seventeenth and twentieth centuries through famous cases of murder and crime. A lot has changed over those 300 years. When the Great Fire ravaged London in 1666, 'the worshipful village of Islington' was a popular tourist resort separated from the bustling City by open fields. Set upon a hill, it boasted fine views of St Paul's and Westminster, clean air, clear water and fine beer. Its attractions included cricket, football, horse-riding, archery, falconry, wrestling and cockfighting. There were also theatrical events featuring clowns, contortionists, strongmen, cannibals, singers and comedians; and lip-smacking offerings of fresh local milk, cheese, custard pies and tea and cake. No wonder Henry VII, Elizabeth I, Sir Walter Raleigh and countless other ladies and gentlemen of the realm were said to favour it as a holiday destination. Samuel Pepys frequently wrote in his diaries of taking his wife and friends on a 'grand tour' of Islington by coach during the evenings, stopping off at the 'Katharine Wheele' and King's Head pubs to gobble down custards and sink as many beers as he pleased. 'And so, we to Islington, and there ate and drank and mighty merry', he wrote in September 1666, 'and so home singing, and after a letter or two at the office, to bed.'

By the end of the nineteenh century Islington was embedded deep within London. Few green fields and open spaces remained as the land became covered with a network of streets, roads, crescents and avenues lined with houses from Angel northwards to Highbury, Finsbury Park, Holloway, Highgate and Crouch Hill. What was once a settlement of only around 300 houses became a crowded borough of more than 200,000 people.

These changes were also reflected in the types of crime committed. In the seventeenh and eighteenth centuries the area was a popular haunt for highwaymen like Claude Duval and Dick Turpin. Robbers lurked in the fields looking for easy prey and pickpockets dipped their way through the crowds at pleasure resorts like Sadler's Musick House and Islington Spa. By the early twentieth century it was the ideal setting for three of the most notorious murder cases in London's history, featuring Dr Crippen, Frederick Seddon and the 'Brides in the Bath' killer George Joseph Smith. This was what George Orwell called 'the Elizabethan period' of English murders, featuring apparently respectable and professional men who felt driven to kill to maintain or advance their position in suburban society. The locations of these crimes are still remembered today.

Case One

# Stand and Deliver

## 1670

Suspect:  Claude Duval

Age:  27

Charge:  Highway Robbery

Sentence:  Execution

London, 2 September 1666. A dark figure in a red silk cloak sits astride his horse at the crest of the hill at Angel Islington and looks down on the city below. It is as if he is gazing into the depths of Hell. Sheets of flame lick the heavens while clouds of smoke and ash billow monstrously from the vast conflagration. It is hard to believe that all this began as a small blaze at a bakery in Pudding Lane. The Great Fire is now spreading in all directions, south to the Thames, east to the Tower, north to the wall at Moorgate and west towards St Paul's. It seems unstoppable.

Most would hesitate before plunging down into the inferno, but the horseman on top of the hill is not afraid. For he is Claude Duval, the most famous highwayman in England, plunderer of men's purses and women's hearts. Earlier that day he had held up a coach carrying the son of the Lord Chief Justice Sir William Morton and his beautiful female companion in Finchley Common. 'Stand and Deliver!' he cried, thrusting two long pistols at his prey, his dark eyes glistening from behind his black mask, his white teeth shining ominously in the moonlight. His reward was bountiful – £400 secreted in a box under the seat. But when the lady offered her diamond necklace, Duval gracefully declined and asked only for a dance. After completing a short courante, he proffered her his ring before vanishing into the night.

The lady who had so enchanted him is now in danger from the raging inferno. Duval races down the hill to Moorfields to rescue her and her mother and then escorts her to the safety of their family home at Highgate. Once there he swoops in for a passionate kiss before revealing his true identity. 'My only prospects are death,' he tells her. 'I am a cheap felon, a thief, an outlaw.'

That is just one of the many stories told about the highwayman who prowled the approaches to London. It comes from Edwin T. Woodhall's book *Claude Duval, Gentleman Highwayman and Knight of the Road*, a fictionalised version of the few facts known about this enthralling figure of history. Almost all that is known about him is found in an anonymous pamphlet printed in 1670, 'The Memoirs of Monsieur Du Vall'. It states that Du Vall was born in Normandy in 1643 and came to England after the Restoration as a servant of 'a person of quality'. He turned to highway robbery mainly to maintain his drinking habit. Although there is no mention of his crimes taking place in Islington, locals honoured him by changing the stretch of road from Lower Holloway to Crouch End from Devil's Lane to Duval's Lane. Perhaps this is proof enough that the 'Knight of the Road' once plied the highway now known as Hornsey Road.

The famous 'courante' with one of his lady victims also appears to have some grounding in fact. According to the memoirs, Duval held up a coach carrying an unnamed knight, his lady, a serving maid and a booty of £400. 'The lady, to shew she was not afraid, takes a flageolet [a wooden flute-type instrument] out of her pocket and plays: Du Vall takes the hint, plays also, and excellently well, upon a flageolet of his own.' Her dancing skills so impressed him that he decided to take only £100 of the £400 available. In this short episode he demonstrated all the qualities that sent English ladies into a swoon:

He manifested his agility of body, by lightly dismounting off his horse, and with ease and freedom getting up again, when he took his leave; his excellent deportment, by his incomparable dancing, and his graceful manner of taking the hundred pounds; his generosity, in taking no more; his wit and eloquence, and readiness at Repartees, in the whole discourse with the Knight and Lady, the greatest part of which I have been forced to omit.

The scene was immortalised by the painter William Powell Frith in 1860.

Yet Duval could also be ruthless. There is an account of him robbing a coach in Blackheath, 'rudely' confiscating their jewellery and even snatching a silver

Claude Duval depicted in a drawing dancing with one of his victims, after the famous painting by William Powell Frith in 1860. (Courtesy of Victorian Picture Library)

suckling bottle from the mouth of a baby. If he was renowned for his courtesy, it was politeness backed up with a loaded pistol. Duval was finally caught by the authorities at the age of twenty-seven. While awaiting execution it is said that 'there were a great company of ladies, and those not of the meanest degree, that visited him in Prison, interceded for his pardon, and accompanied him to the gallows'. The legend has it that after his execution at Tyburn on 21 January 1670, his body was cut down from the gallows and laid 'in state' at the Tangier tavern in St Giles, before being buried 'in the middle isle in Covent-Garden Church, under a plain white marble stone, whereon are curiously engraved the Du Vall's arms, and, under them, written in black, this epitaph' [sic]:

Here lies Du Vall: Reader, if Male thou art,
Look to thy Purse; if Female, to thy Heart.
Much havoc has he made of both; for all
Men he made stand, and Women he made fall
The Second Conqueror of the Norman Race,
Knights to his Arms did yield, and Ladies to his Face.
Old Tyburn's Glory; England's illustrious Thief,
Du Vall, the Ladies' Joy; Du Vall, the Ladies' Grief.

Modern retellings of the Duval legend suggest he was buried at St Paul's Church in Covent Garden. But this is yet another London myth that was probably started by Walter Thornbury in his *Old and New London*. St Paul's confirm that there is no record of his burial there and certainly no grave marker. Edwin Woodhall's fictional account suggests that it was St Giles' Church, but if this is true no trace remains, as it was rebuilt in the early eighteenth century. It is thought the most likely explanation is that Duval was buried unromantically in a pauper's grave at Tyburn. Often truth is duller than fiction.

Many other highwaymen, now long forgotten, plied their trade on the 'Great North Road' from the city to the provinces via the villages of Islington and Highgate. Few lived up to the example of the gallant rogue Duval, not least because they were often too poor to afford horses and prowled the area by foot. At the Old Bailey in 1675 five such 'footpads' were condemned to death for their crimes. 'Their usual practice was to lurk in the Evening, or very early in the Morning, about Islington, and other skirts of the Town,' it was recorded, 'and force what single Passenger they could meet with to surrender their Purses, and sometimes with sudden violence took Contribution of Hats and Cloaks, one of them had the good luck to meet with a Booty of Thirty and odd pounds, though now he is likely to pay dear enough for the Purchase.' In another case from 1692 a gang of seven or eight highwaymen stopped the coach of John Lacey Esq. 'a little beyond Islington' as he made his way to Tottenham High Cross with his wife and maid. Their reward was a gold watch, a pair of diamond pendants and fine clothing worth more than £80. Only one suspect was convicted and condemned to death, a soldier from Islington called John Neale.

At a time when there was no police force worthy of the name, it is likely that only a very small proportion of highway robbers were ever prosecuted. However, the cases that did go to court reveal some of the methods used to combat them. In 1683 a group of Islington residents were notified that two suspects were en route from Highgate and so they lay in wait. The trap was successful, but only after one of the locals was shot dead during the pursuit. It was also not unknown for the victims to fight back, sometimes with surprising success. In 1715 a traveller passing through Holloway managed to fight off two armed robbers using a stick in one hand and a knife in the other. One of the attackers died of his injuries and the second was let off with a fine of £50, possibly because he had already been punished with a stab wound to the belly.

Case Two

# Dick Turpin

1739

Suspect:    Dick Turpin

Age:        34

Charge:     Horse Stealing

Sentence:   Execution

The most famous highwayman of them all arrived in Islington on Sunday 22 May 1737. Dick Turpin quickly wreaked havoc among the coaches and carriages on the roads around Holloway and Highgate, depriving one travelling gentleman after another of their money. At midday, according to newspaper reports, he ventured down Back Lane (now Liverpool Road) and held up two men in a chaise. One of them dared to suggest to Turpin that he had reigned long enough and would soon be captured. To which Turpin replied, ''Tis no matter for that, I am not afraid of being taken by you, therefore don't stand hesitating, but give me the Cole.' With that he seized a purse of guineas and rode off.

Turpin was by then the most wanted man in England. For the previous two years he had been rampaging through the counties surrounding London – Essex, Middlesex, Surrey and Kent – robbing, housebreaking and stealing whatever he could find. Turpin seems to have started out by stealing bullocks in Plaistow in 1733 at the age of twenty-eight, before joining smugglers near Canvey Island. He then fell in with 'Gregory's gang' in Essex, at first helping them to dispose of stolen deer and later with burglaries and raids around Epping Forest, Chingford, Woodford and Barking. They became so notorious that the authorities offered £50 a head for their capture. 'Richard Turpin', the notice read:

A butcher by trade, is a tall fresh coloured man, very much marked with the small pox, about twenty-six years of age, about five feet nine inches high, lived some time ago in Whitechapel and did lately lodge somewhere about Millbank, Westminster, wears a blue grey coat and a light natural wig.

After several members were captured and the ringleader Samuel Gregory was executed at Tyburn in June 1735, Turpin embarked on highway robbery. His favourite hunting grounds are said to have been Epping Forest, Finchley Common, Hounslow Heath, Hampstead Heath and Enfield, but he was not afraid to try his hand south of the river near Kingston, Putney, Wandsworth, Barnes and Blackheath. Hackney and Islington became more popular targets in late 1736 and early 1737, possibly because they were close to his safe house, the Red Lion tavern, near Hatton Garden, whose landlord is said to have been one of the most notorious fences in London. One story is that Turpin stopped a man near Hackney and demanded his money, only for the victim to reveal that he was poor and only carrying 18*d*. Turpin and his gang gave him half a crown and set off for richer pickings in Islington. On the way they held up a gentleman and stole his gold repeater pistol before returning to the Red Lion. By March 1737 he was known as 'the famous Turpin, who rides with an open gold lace hat'.

On 4 May that year, two weeks before turning up in Islington Back Lane, he or one of his accomplices shot a man dead in Epping Forest. A proclamation was issued stating that:

> Whereas it has been represented to the King that Richard Turpin on Wednesday the Fourth of May last did barbarously murder Thomas Morris, servant to Henry Thompson, one of the Keepers of Epping Forest … his Majesty for better discovering and bringing the said Richard Turpin to justice is pleased to promise his most gracious pardon to any one of the accomplices of the said Richard Turpin who shall discover him so that he may be apprehended and convicted.

The reward was £200. Turpin was this time described as being: 'about five feet nine inches high, of a brown complexion very much marked with the small pox. His cheek bones broad. His face thinner towards the bottom. His visage short. Pretty upright and broad about the shoulders.' With a heavy price on his head, he left London and headed north.

Turpin leaping the Horsey gate; illustration by Cruickshank in William Harrison Ainsworth's Rookwood. (Author)

Dick Turpin's ride to York upon his faithful steed Black Bess is the most famous of all his exploits. It is also fiction. In 1834 William Harrison Ainsworth published *Rookwood*, a historical romance that cast Turpin as a romantic hero. It was so successful that the story of Turpin's twenty-four-hour ride to York became meshed together with the true story of his life. In *Rookwood*, Turpin fled his pursuers from Kilburn up Shoot-Up Hill Lane (now Edgware Road) towards Hampstead, then crossed to Highgate and then on to Hornsey and Duval's Lane in Crouch End. 'The men of Hornsey rushed into the road to seize the fugitive, and women held up their babes to catch a glimpse of the flying cavalcade,' wrote Ainsworth. Turpin evaded the chasing pack by leaping the high turnpike gate, and galloped on through Tottenham, Edmonton, Enfield and up through Huntingdon, Grantham and Bawtry. Just as he caught sight of the towers and pinnacles of York for the first time, his horse Bess met her own tragic but heroic end, collapsing and dying of exhaustion.

The novel spawned many imitations. In 1839, Henry Downes Miles wrote *The Life of Richard Palmer*, which also featured a fictional ride to York. This time Turpin hurtled up the Goswell Road towards the Angel at Islington.

The gravelled road rung loudly to the rattling gallop of the gallant Bess, and the bright sparks flew brilliantly from the flints imbedded in the drift; for the unfrequent carriage traffic allowed such soft material to be used to bind the large coarse gravel with which the highway was repaired.

In the book, Turpin stops at an 'old fashioned hostel' at Angel and downs one glass of brandy after another. As he dispatches his fifth shot, he hears his pursuers churn up the City Road, throws a guinea on the bar and takes off, telling the landlord to 'keep the change until Dick Turpin returns'.

Although this legendary twenty-four-hour ride never happened, the real Dick Turpin did end up settling in York as John Palmer. In October 1738 he was arrested for shooting his landlord's cock in the street and locked up after failing to find a surety for bail. He was only identified as Dick Turpin when he wrote to his brother-in-law asking for money for bail. Yet he would be hauled before the courts for horse stealing rather than highway robbery or murder, not that it really mattered – the punishment was still death by hanging. On the day of his execution, 7 April 1739, dressed in a new frock coat and shoes and flanked by hired mourners, he flung himself from the gallows rather than waiting for the drop.

The death of Black Bess, illustration from Rookwood. (Author)

Case Three

# The Thief-taker

## 1723

Suspect:     Jonathan Wild
Age:         Unknown
Charge:      Prison Breaking
             & Theft

Sentence:    Execution

The 'golden age' of highwaymen during the late seventeenth and early eighteenth centuries led to the development of new types of policing. One of these was the 'thief-taker' who tracked down criminals and stolen loot in return for large rewards. The most notorious of them all was Jonathan Wild, a godfather-type figure who won the admiration of the country for his ability to catch criminals and to restore stolen goods to their rightful owners.

On 30 August 1721, Wild successfully prosecuted two footpads from Islington on the testimony of their criminal colleagues. The first, a forty-year-old plasterer called John Wigley, was convicted of stealing a silver watch and spurs from a gentleman in Islington even though the victim could not identify him as the robber. The crucial evidence came from Jonathan Wild and the hardened criminal William Burridge. 'Jonathan Wild deposed that Burridge told him that the prisoner, James Shaw and himself did the Fact. The Prisoner denied the Fact and said that it was a malicious Prosecution in Burridge.' Wigley was convicted and executed the following week, having confessed to carrying out 'many robberies' in Islington. The second, thirty-five-year-old James Reading, was one of three footpads who jumped out of a ditch, pulled George Brownsworth off his horse and made off with his watch, silver spurs, silver buckles and two guineas. Burridge testified that he, Reading and Shaw carried out the robbery together and Reading was duly executed in September 1721.

Both of these cases illustrate the sayings 'No honour among thieves' and 'Thieves never prosper'. They also demonstrate that testifying for Wild was no guarantee that you would escape the dock. Before his arrest, James Reading testified against four other criminals and implicated Shaw in at least one robbery. Five months after Reading's execution Shaw, twenty-eight, was himself sentenced to death for the murder of Philip Potts during a robbery in the parish of St Pancras (which was also said to involve Reading). A month after that Burridge was executed for stealing a horse.

Jonathan Wild being pelted with stones and dirt on the way to the gallows at Tyburn in the back of a cart. (Author)

In truth, Wild's empire was corrupt to the core; he orchestrated the robberies, kept the stolen goods and after a time returned them to the owners to claim the reward. If any of his thieves turned against him or failed to give him a share of the loot he would pursue them to the gallows. Wild, who lived down the road from the Old Bailey, effectively controlled all crime in London. But eventually he too met a gruesome end – in May 1725 Wild was prosecuted for stealing 50 yards of lace from a shopkeeper and then claiming the reward of ten guineas for returning it. Three months later he was hanged at Tyburn in front of a huge crowd, including the authors Daniel Defoe and Henry Fielding.

Twenty-four years later, Henry Fielding and his brother John founded the Bow Street Runners, London's first professional police force. Then in 1755, John Fielding published his 'plan for preventing robberies within twenty miles of London'. Fielding complained that while more robberies took place within 20 miles of London than in the whole country, 'not one in a hundred of these robbers are taken in the fact'. His solution was the creation of horse patrols;

Drawing of the Red Lion, from Walter Thornbury's
Old and New London. (Author)

'always ready to pursue and attack the most daring villain'. At first these
patrols monitored the popular places of entertainment, but by 1763 they circled
the whole of London from Pimlico to Highgate and back again via Fulham,
Hammersmith, Ealing, Paddington, Shoreditch, Whitechapel, Greenwich,
Clapham and Wandsworth. Unfortunately, the treasury withdrew its funding
the following year and the highwaymen returned; the Prime Minister Lord
North, the Prince of Wales, and the Duke of York were all robbed on the roads
in the 1770s, but the patrols were not brought back until 1805. By then a
series of police stations had been established around London, a further step on
the slow evolution towards the Metropolitan Police, established in 1829.

Memories of Jonathan Wild and Dick Turpin were stirred again more than
a century after their deaths when demolition workers began clearing old
houses in West Street, Clerkenwell, for the building of Farringdon Lane. In
one of them they found evidence that it had been used as a thieves' den. 'It
has all the conveniences of a hiding place, with concealed means of escape

in dark closets, sliding panels and secret recesses, and by as many trap doors as in the stage of a theatre,' claimed the *Illustrated London News* on 17 August 1844. Crowds gathered at the scene to see for themselves how wanted men of old had evaded the authorities by climbing through a window, crossing the Fleet Ditch over a plank and disappearing down Black Boy Alley and Cow Cross.

It was claimed that the building at No. 3 West Street (formerly Chick Lane) was once the Red Lion, the reputed haunt of Dick Turpin. According to the *Examiner* newspaper,

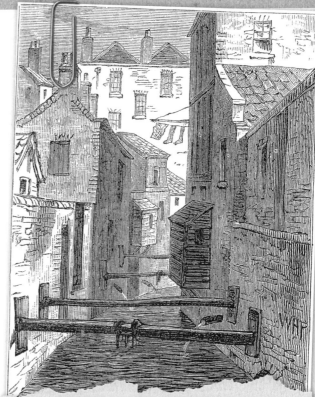

View over the Fleet Ditch from the rear of the Old Red Lion, from Old and New London. (Author)

the tavern was built by the chief of a tribe of gypsies as a front for their criminal activities, including handling stolen goods and harbouring convicted thieves. Down in the foundations, labourers uncovered two male skeletons, who 'must have become the victims of the wretches who inhabit this den of infamy and after being murdered, thrown through a trapdoor immediately over the spot'.

Another account suggested that No. 3 West Street was used by the thief-taker Jonathan Wild himself, on the evidence of an old rusty knife found in one of the rooms. According to the *Illustrated London News*, the blade bore the name of Rippam, and the handle 'J. Wilde'. *Lloyd's Weekly Newspaper*, on the other hand, claimed that, 'An old rusty pronged fork, with a silver handle, evidently of very ancient manufacture, was found in the lower part of the premises.' It was taken to Clerkenwell Police Court and presented for inspection on the basis that 'it was found in Jonathan Wild's old house in West Street'.

The *Examiner* reported: 'we can find no account of its being the residence of Jonathan Wild, his houses being in the Old Bailey and Wych Street. There is not the slightest doubt, however, that it was one of his principal hoards.'

Yet another account suggested it was a hiding place of Jack Sheppard, a prolific thief and burglar who achieved fame by escaping from prison four times (St Giles' Roundhouse, Clerkenwell New Prison, and Newgate Prison twice). Sheppard was only twenty-two when he was executed at Tyburn on 16 November 1724, having been convicted at the Old Bailey of housebreaking and theft of 118 yards of woollen cloth. The key witness for the prosecution was Jonathan Wild.

# A Duel

## 1712

Suspect:     Patrick French
Age:         Unknown
Charge:      Murder
Sentence:    Found not guilty

On 14 August 1712, a lieutenant in the Royal Navy decided to spend the evening at the theatre. The establishment that Mr Ingram Thwaits chose was one of the most notorious in London: Sadler's Wells, otherwise known as Miles' Musick House. Here the paying customer could enjoy all manner of debauchery from drinking and feasting to dancing and fornication. A few years earlier it had been the scene for one of the most disgusting performances ever staged, when the so-called 'Hibernian Canibal' ate a whole live cockerel in front of a baying – and vomiting – crowd.

He catch'd him behind the Gills, and snap'd off his Head with as much Slight and Expedition, as a New-England Hog will an Acorn from a Dwarf-Oake, cracking the Skull as nimbly, to come at the Brains, as a Squirrel does a Nutshell, to come at the Kernel; then dipping on't in a Platter of Sawce, gave it all Mastication together, except the Beak, and down he swallow'd it, Feathers and all, that it might sit the lighter upon his Stomach: Then he clap'd the Fundament to his Mouth, and dragging out several Yards of Guts, he laid those by him, to East at last; as People do Cheese for Digestion.

Sadler's Wells in 1756, from Old and New London. (Author)

The theatre was notorious not only because of the entertainment but also the clientele. Mr Thwaits sat in his box in the Gallery with his bottle of cider, would have had a fine view of the cheap seats in the 'Pit' below:

> Where Butchers and Bailiffs, and such sort of Fellows,
> Were mix'd with a Vermin train'd up to the Gallows;
> As Buttocks and Files, Housebreakers and Padders,
> With Prize-Fighters, Sweetners, and such sort of Traders,
> Informers, Thief-Takers, Deer-Stealers and Bullies,
> Old Straw-Hatted Whores, with their Twelve-Penny Cullies,
> Some Dancing & Skipping, some Ranting & Tearing
> Some Drinking and Smoking, some Lying and Swearing

>        From 'A Walk to Islington' (1699)

But Mr Thwaits would not live to see the last act that night. After leaving his box briefly during the performance, he returned to find it had been occupied by Patrick French, a lawyer from Clerkenwell. The stand-off quickly deteriorated into a deadly duel:

> Mr Thwaits thereupon demanded his Place, which Mr French readily resign'd; but said afterwards, if he had thought it was not his Place, he would not have parted with it so easily; whereupon Mr Thwaits reply'd, He was a foolish Fellow to think he'd tell him a Lye; immediately upon which, Mr French clapt his Hand upon his Sword, and drew it part out, and then Mr Thwaits and he drew both, and made four or five Passes at each other, and Mr Thwaits fell.

Thwaits, his heart pierced, bled to death within seconds.

A month later French was put on trial at the Old Bailey for murder. He did not deny inflicting the injury but claimed that he had been trying to defend himself. Mr Thwaits was the aggressor and had been the first to draw a weapon, he told the court, and forced him into a corner from which there was no escape. According to Patrick French, he had little choice but to drive his blade into the lieutenant's chest to a depth of six inches. French also called witnesses to say that the victim was an ill-tempered, quarrelsome man whereas he, French, was 'a very quiet honest Gentleman, and of very inoffensive conversation.' French was acquitted by the jury and walked out a free man.

Case Five

# The Cricket Field

### 1797

Suspect:     Martin Clinch &

              James Mackley

Age:         22

Charge:     Highway Robbery & Murder

Sentence:    Execution

It was a pleasant Sunday evening on 7 May 1797, when Sydney Fryer, a young lawyer and 'gentleman of considerable property', set off with his cousin Ann from Southampton buildings at the junction between Holborn and Chancery Lane. Their destination was Islington, up Grays Inn Lane towards Mount Pleasant, the Clerkenwell House of Correction and the edge of the city. Taking the path north from Baynes Row (now Exmouth Street) would have taken them across open fields to a pleasure garden called 'Merlin's Cave', thought to have been built in imitation of an entertainment created at George II's royal gardens at Richmond in 1735. To the right was the New River Head, Islington Spa and Sadler's Wells, and to the left across the fields was Bagnigge Wells. The path continued to the reservoir and the New Road. Here they would have briefly been plunged back into an urban landscape as they made their way up Penton Street towards White Conduit House, a popular working-class attraction boasting tree-lined walks, bowling greens, Dutch-pin grounds, boxing matches, a fish pond and a tea house offering buttered rolls and cream.

Behind the house and gardens (which used to stand roughly at the junction of Barnsbury Road and Dewey Road) there was the cricket field, former home of the White Conduit Club which moved to Marylebone and became the

Drawing of White Conduit House in around 1820, from Old and New London. (Author)

Drawing of White Conduit House from 1731, viewed from the south, in Pinks' History of Clerkenwell.

Islington in 1780, from Old and New London. (Author)

MCC in 1787. The path then took Mr Fryer and his cousin through open land towards the 'Workhouse Field', so-called because of the workhouse just north of what is now Barnsbury Street. It was here, about three quarters of a mile north of White Conduit House, that Sydney and Ann Fryer heard the sound of a woman in distress.

'I observed to Mr Fryer that I heard a noise ... from the right-hand side,' said Ann Fryer. 'He stopped with me to listen and said "There is", and immediately went over the stile.' She followed him and saw a man on the other side with a silk handkerchief covering the lower half of his face. Sydney Fryer asked what he was doing. The man's response was to raise a pistol to Fryer's head and pull the trigger. There was a flash and a bang and Sydney Fryer fell down into a small pond, a bullet wound just above his left temple. The gunman then calmly went through the stricken Mr Fryer's pockets, pulled out a watch, and advanced towards Ann.

'He came up to me with a pistol, and desired me to deliver my money,' she recalled. 'My hand trembled and I could not get to my pocket. He said "Make haste, give me your money", and I gave him my purse.' A second man appeared and demanded she hand over her black silk cloak. The two robbers then fled.

Ann Fryer ran across the fields to get help at the King's Arms in Park Place (now Islington Park Street). The landlord, William Rise, roused his neighbours and led them into the fields to collect the injured victim and search for the robbers. It was too late for Mr Fryer – he died two hours later at around eleven o'clock. The culprits had also long since disappeared.

Nine days later, a tip-off led to the arrest of gambling addict and bookbinder Martin Clinch at the Weavers Arms near Finsbury Square. The following evening James Mackley, a printer with the Logographic Press, was taken at the Magpie & Stump in Sun Street, Finsbury. When they were hauled before Worship Street Police Court, Ann Fryer fixed her gaze upon them and declared that Clinch was the first robber and Mackley the man who took her cloak. Giving evidence at the Old Bailey, she repeated her identification of Clinch, pointing him out in the dock. 'The shortest man in the blue coat, I believe, from my soul, to be the man.' As for the second robber, she stated that Mackley 'resembles him in his person', even though she never saw his face.

The only support for her claims was a sighting of two men in the fields about 200 yards from the scene of the murder, just over an hour before Sydney Fryer was shot. Descriptions of the men varied. Elizabeth Goddard, who was walking through the area with her husband and two sons, described one man as having 'carrotty hair' like Mackley's, and the other as wearing a brown coat and a light waistcoat, but was not prepared to positively identify either prisoner. Her husband Robert said the prisoners 'very much resembled' the two men in the fields but added, 'I am not confident whether those men are the men.' Their eldest son Robert positively identified Clinch, but thirteen-year-old George Goddard told the court that he had not taken much notice of them and could not help the court either way. However, he did reveal that on his way back home alone from White Conduit House he had seen the same two men sat only 10 yards from the stile where the murder was committed.

The jury were not told that Clinch had been tried for another highway robbery just three months earlier, only to be acquitted after the witness stated he could not be certain of his attackers. Similar problems with witness identification afflicted this case. Could Ann Fryer be certain who was responsible, given her distress at witnessing her cousin's cold-blooded murder? The judge, Mr Justice Grose, declared that:

Undoubtedly, if you believe the witnesses, it clearly appears that Clinch is the man who committed the fact, and the other is the man who is stated to have been present at the time … it will be for you to judge whether a better and more distinct account could be given by a female, under the circumstance in which she was, and under which she had now been examined.

Half an hour later, Clinch and Mackley were found guilty of murder and sentenced to death at the age of twenty-two. Clinch thanked the court for the fairness of the trial but insisted that he was no more guilty of murder than Miss Fryer.

Those looking for a sign that an injustice had been done would have been satisfied by the botched nature of the execution. For as Clinch and Mackley waited for the caps to be drawn over their eyes, the entire wooden platform suddenly collapsed. The executioner, his assistant, Clinch's Catholic priest and Mackley's Protestant clergyman were all sent crashing to the ground, while the condemned men felt the noose tighten around their necks much earlier than they expected. But the end result was the same and both of their bodies were taken off to be publicly displayed at Apothecaries' Hall not far from the Old Bailey. Then, as was the custom, they were dissected.

Despite the verdict, it was widely believed that Clinch and Mackley were both innocent of the crime. The *Newgate Calendar* reported:

When the two men died most of the people were of opinion that their fate was just; but soon after the confessions of three separate criminals, who could have had no interest in taking the crime upon themselves, threw a different light upon the transaction, and recalled to mind the strong assertions which Clinch and Mackley had made of their innocence.

# Clowns and Robbers

| | |
|---|---|
| *Suspect:* | *Robert Goodwin & Dennis Green* |
| *Age:* | *20 & 19* |
| *Charge:* | *Housebreaking* |
| *Sentence:* | *Execution, commuted to transportation for life* |

In a small public park just off the Pentonville Road there is a gravestone surrounded by black railings decorated with the masks of Comedy and Tragedy. A plaque set into the ground reveals that it is the resting place of Joseph Grimaldi, the greatest clown that ever lived and a genuine Clerkenwell celebrity. From his first performance at Sadler's Wells at the age of three, to his retirement at forty-six, he could 'fill a theatre anywhere' with physical comedy, costume changes, pantomime dames and songs that had the audience rolling in the aisles.

Grimaldi, or just plain 'Joey', was also a master of the anecdote. Many of his tales can be found in his memoirs, edited by none other than Charles Dickens and published in 1838, a year after Grimaldi's death.

One of these stories involves his encounter with a notorious gang of thieves he called the 'Pentonville Robbers'. At the end of the eighteenth century, Pentonville was a small, pleasant suburb set in the fields of Islington, bounded by White

*Joseph Grimaldi's gravestone at Joseph Grimaldi Park off Pentonville Road. (Author)*

Grimaldi's debut at Sadler's Wells in 1782 'in the arduous character of a monkey', drawn by George Cruickshank for Grimaldi, edited by Boz.

Conduit House and Sadler's Wells Theatre. It made an attractive target for burglars and the Pentonville Robbers had at one point been twenty strong. By 1797 most of the gang had been captured and executed or transported to Australia, but three or four of them remained at large. Grimaldi, aged eighteen and yet to make his name, was living with his mother in Penton Place, now Penton Rise, opposite the old burial ground which later became the public park that bears his name. It was August and the clown was rehearsing his latest show. On his return home, his mother noticed the garden gate was open. 'Oh dear me!' she exclaimed. 'How careless this is?' Approaching the house, she noticed that the front door was also ajar and caught a reflection of light at the end of the passage. After screaming for help, she bravely went down the stairs and found her home had been ransacked of almost everything of value.

'The house was in a state of great disorder and confusion, but no thieves were to be seen,' remembered Grimaldi. 'The cupboards were forced, the drawers had been broken open, and every article they contained had been removed.' Grabbing an old broadsword hung from a peg, he crept into the darkness of the back garden and climbed the wall to try and intercept the robbers as they made their escape. Grimaldi spotted one of the gang about to climb down into the pasture behind the house. 'Hush, hush, is that you?' asked the robber, mistaking the clown for one of his colleagues.

'Yes,' Grimaldi replied, moving closer before swinging his mighty weapon. Yelping in pain, the thief fell to the ground, blood oozing from his leg, before jumping up and limping away. Determined to apprehend the criminal, Grimaldi leapt down after him and gave chase, only to tumble acrobatically over a cow lying on the ground. He would later boast that he might have cut his own head off with the sword had it not been for his theatrical training as a fencer. Giving up the pursuit, Grimaldi returned to the house to work out what had been stolen.

The most heartbreaking loss was his treasured insect collection, including a cabinet of Adonis blue butterflies which he had gathered during night-time flits to Dartford in Kent. It now lay smashed upon the floor, irreparably damaged. Grimaldi was so devastated that he gave up the hobby and turned to pigeon fancying instead.

He was to have his revenge on the Pentonville Robbers two weeks later, after the gang made a second unsuccessful attempt to raid the house. With the help of a local parish constable named Trott, he laid a trap to catch them when they returned for a third time in search of even more loot. Sure enough, two men picked the lock and entered the house while the clown and his family were out at the theatre.

'Wouldn't you like to know who it was as struck you with the sword, Tom?' one of them asked.

'I wish I did, I'd put a knife in him before many days was over.'

Trott then sprang the trap, locking the front door and firing a pistol down the stairs to signal to his two colleagues to come out and arrest the thieves. Their fate was to be transported for life, while Grimaldi moved to a safer location in Penton Street.

Charles Dickens saw this episode as:

> … a striking and curious picture of the state of society in and about London, in this respect, at the very close of the last century. The bold and daring highwaymen … had ceased to canter their blood-horses over heath and road in search of plunder, but there still existed in the capital and its environs, common and poorer gangs of thieves, whose depredations were conducted with a daring and disregard of consequences which to the citizens of this age is wholly extraordinary.

Dickens also suggested that if this episode had taken place in 1838 instead of 1797, it would have 'set all London, and all the country for thirty miles round to boot, in a ferment of wonder and indignation'.

It seems likely the story of the Pentonville Robbers is either vastly exaggerated or entirely made up, because it is difficult to find any references to the Pentonville Robbers in contemporary reports, despite claims to their notoriety. It is possible he was basing his account on a burglary of No. 58 Penton Street in the early hours of 21 May 1792, when John Ball and his brother Joshua broke into the home of Ann Farrer through the back kitchen window. They snatched not only the silver spoons and sugar tongs but also boots, shoes, stockings, aprons, sheets, tablecloths and a ¼lb of tea. Fortunately for Mrs Farrer, the burglars were spotted running across the field with their loot by a watchman and were arrested near Tottenham Court Road.

Joseph Grimaldi the clown performing in the pantomime Harlequin and Friar Bacon, from Pinks' History of Clerkenwell.

Both were found guilty and transported to Australia for seven years. Perhaps the closest real-life matches to the 'Pentonville Robbers' are Robert Goodwin and Dennis Green, who lived in Dobney's (or Daubigney's) Place off Penton Street in 1800. At two o'clock in the morning on 22 February, they broke into the home of a local gentleman, Benjamin Holdsworth, and stole 45s worth of silver cutlery as well as various pieces of clothing, linen cloths and napkins, and 3lb of bacon. The crime was only discovered by a servant the next morning. Goodwin and Green might have got away with it had it not been for an honest pawnbroker, William Crouch of Ray Street, Clerkenwell. After being offered a silver toast rack and a pair of silver sugar tongs for 14s, Mr Crouch became suspicious when he spotted the owner's crest. Goodwin, aged twenty, and Green, aged nineteen, were arrested, and the stolen silver was discovered in a hole in the wall of their room. Both were found guilty of burglary and condemned to death, although their sentences were reduced to transportation for life. Green ended up as a successful farmer in New South Wales, Australia, and had seven children before passing away in 1855.

As for Joseph Grimaldi, he left Penton Street following the death of his wife in October 1799 and moved to Baynes Row, Clerkenwell. He found fame in 1806 with his performance in the play *Mother Goose* and established the archetype of the 'white-faced clown'.

His career finally came to an end with a 'farewell benefit' at Drury Lane theatre in 1828. Seven years later, after spending several years living in Woolwich, he returned to Pentonville to spend the last two years of his life at No. 33 Southampton Street (now renamed Calshot Street). Grimaldi did not mention it in his memoirs, but this road had only a few months earlier been the scene of the horrific murder of a young mother and her four young children.

SOLVED

# The House of Blood

## 1834

| | |
|---|---|
| *Suspect:* | *Mr John Steinberg* |
| *Age:* | *45* |
| *Charge:* | *Infanticide, Filicide & Murder* |
| *Sentence:* | *Felo de se* |

At six o'clock in the morning on Tuesday 9 September 1834, a fifteen-year-old servant girl walked up Southampton Street in Pentonville and knocked on the front door of No. 17. Harriet Pearson had arrived on time, just as Mr and Mrs Steinberg had requested, but there was no answer. She knocked again. All was quiet. She could not even hear the cries of the couple's baby son, or their three other children. Uncertain what to do next, Harriet hung about the house for nigh on three hours in case they did not want to be disturbed at such an early hour after all. Finally, at nine o'clock, with the house remaining unusually quiet for such a young family, she decided to return to her mother's home in Edmond Street in Battle Bridge. It was autumn and the leaves on the trees were turning red and brown and falling mournfully into the streets.

An hour later, accompanied by her mother, Harriet returned. Again there was no answer. Mrs Pearson adventurously clambered over the wall into the yard to try the back door, but it was locked. It was only at eleven o'clock that the landlord, Lewis Cuthbert, arrived, alerted by a neighbour who suspected that the Steinbergs had fled without paying the rent. He forced open the door and gazed in horror at the scene within. 'I saw Mr Steinberg lying at full length on the kitchen floor. There was a great deal of blood about his clothes and the place, and his throat was horribly cut.' Mr Cuthbert immediately called in the police.

Upstairs, the first floor was even more hellish. In the main bedroom they found a woman they believed to be Mrs Steinberg lying face down on the floor in her nightdress. Her head was nearly severed from her body, so deep was the gash to her throat. At her feet was her youngest, Philip, eight months old, decapitated. The bed, bedclothes, and the pillow, were all stained red with blood. The second floor was a fresh nightmare. By the side of a cot lay Ellen, two years old, with her throat cut from ear to ear. Her five-year-old brother Henry had been just as cruelly dispatched in his own bed. In the next room, four-year-old John had obviously put up a fight. One of the fingers on his left hand had been cut off and there was a deep gash in his right shoulder. But John too had succumbed to the same cruel end as the rest of his family.

The Metropolitan Police, only five years old itself, did not take long to conclude that there was no homicidal maniac loose on the streets. All the evidence pointed to the dead father – John Nicholas Steinberg, a forty-five-year-old whip maker from Germany. The doors of the house were all locked, there were no signs of a robbery and the murder weapon lay by his side. According to a local tradesman, he had bought the white-handled butcher's knife on Monday 8th. On the kitchen table lay a blank piece of paper, a pen and ink, as if Steinberg had intended to write a note explaining his actions, only to be overwhelmed by the horror of what he had just done.

Word swept the neighbourhood and by the afternoon 'the crowd was so dense and anxious that the street was rendered impassable' and the police struggled to keep the masses away from the house. Another report claimed: 'the interest was so great that persons of the utmost respectability, amongst whom were many eminent surgeons, attended at the house begging for admission, but they were denied.' The throng were horrified, excited, tearful and angry as they heard descriptions of the attractive twenty-five-year-old mother and her children lying in a house so stained and spattered it resembled 'one mass of human blood'.

The crowds were still there when the sixteen members of the jury hearing the inquest were taken to view the scene at five o'clock in the afternoon the next day. As *The Times* newspaper put it: 'the appearance of the mutilated bodies created a painful sensation in the breast of the jury and every person present.' One of the jurors was so distressed that they had to retire before hearing further evidence at the Vernon Arms pub in Pentonville Road. As witness after witness told of their dealings with Mr Steinberg, a picture emerged of a troubled man driven to the depths of despair.

The main revelation was that the dead young woman at No. 17 Southampton Street was not Mrs Steinberg at all – her name was Ellen Lefevre, and the real Mrs Steinberg was living with her husband's nineteen-year-old son, Nicholas, at a house in Leigh Street, Burton Crescent, St Pancras. It appeared that ten years earlier, John Steinberg and his wife had taken pity on fifteen-year-old Ellen, the daughter of a failed bookseller who hanged himself on Primrose Hill, and offered her a job as their servant girl. It was rumoured that Steinberg had seduced the teenager during regular outings to see his son at a boarding school in Hampstead. When Mrs Steinberg found out, she threw Ellen out of the house and tried to stop the lovers from seeing each other. It did not work. John Steinberg walked out on his existing family to start a new one with his teenage mistress at an ironmonger's home in Hampstead Road. After the birth of their first child, Henry, they moved first to Chelsea, and finally to Southampton Street in the summer of 1833.

Opinions of John Steinberg varied wildly, depending on who you talked to and on what particular subject. Neighbours knew him as 'a man of very retired habits', and a 'highly respectable tradesman', who was said to own a patent on a whip 'of peculiar construction'. His estranged wife, when contacted by reporters, spoke highly of her husband and the maintenance he paid of £2 10s a quarter. His teenage son, on the other hand, believed him to be insane. 'My father was of a very irritable and passionate disposition, and every circumstance agitated and affected his mind,' Nicholas Steinberg told the inquest. 'My father used me severely and beat me often. He used my mother very ill, struck her, and beat her once almost to death.'

According to the servant girl, Harriet Pearson, Steinberg behaved very affectionately towards his new partner but did not always treat their young children so tenderly. Harriet told the jury that:

My master was a very passionate man. When he was in a passion I have seen him pull his children up by the hair of their heads and ears and throw them down. My mistress used to pull him away mildly, and remonstrate with him, and say if they deserved beating, it should be elsewhere.

One of Steinberg's employees defended his master by saying that he only beat the children with a whip when they deserved it.

A few months before the murders, on 21 May, Steinberg took his family and their servant girl to Germany to visit an ill relative and to collect a debt he believed was owed him for a number of whips. During their journey back to England, he complained to a fellow passenger, Fritz Langar, about losing a law suit, which cost him £200. On top of that, his sister had charged him for board and lodging during their stay. Langar described him as appearing 'almost insane'. Steinberg's mood didn't improve when he returned home on Saturday 6 September to find that his business had been neglected by the young whip maker he had left in charge, Brockhart Brunish. Mr Brunish was so fearful of arrest that he did not even dare to visit the house to collect the two sovereigns that he was owed for his work. Then on Monday evening, Steinberg met Fritz Langar for a drink at the King of Prussia pub in Lambeth Street in Whitechapel. Mr Langar told the inquest: 'He threw himself in all sorts of attitudes and said he was ruined. He pulled out some papers, and in his side pocket I perceived a long parcel, which I have no doubt was a knife.'

The last person to see the family alive was Harriet Pearson on the Monday night at half eight. After fetching a pint of beer and a quartern of gin for supper, and seeing the children to bed, she overheard Steinberg asking Ellen Lefevre if she wanted to retire for the night. Ellen replied that it was too early. Steinberg told her to give Harriet a raspberry cake. The servant girl was paid her wages and sent home on the promise that she would be back at six o'clock the next morning. 'I saw no difference in his manner on the evening that I last saw him,' she said. Perhaps he had already decided on the crime.

Journalists reported that the jury room was 'literally besieged' by the curious and excitable crowds hoping to discover what had caused Steinberg to murder his partner and children in cold blood. At half past eleven, the jury returned a verdict of *felo de se*, a legal term for suicide which translates as 'felon of himself'. Steinberg's property was to be forfeited to the Crown and his body buried according to custom – usually at a crossroads with a stake driven through the heart.

On the night of Thursday 11 September, Steinberg's body was taken to the paupers' burial ground in Ray Street, Clerkenwell. Attempts to keep the funeral a secret were unsuccessful, and a crowd quickly gathered to shout insults at the dead man.

According to one account:

A party of men with lighted flambeaux led the officers and bearers of the deceased's body to a deep hole about eighteen or twenty feet deep. After exhibiting it to the public view it was taken out of the shell and pitched headlong into it, and the hollow sound of the body when it went to the bottom was shocking, and excited a feeling of horror; but in the grave the men with the links shook them over the body, and made contemptuous remarks with the greatest levity. The windows looking into the churchyard were crowded by persons, who cried out 'Why don't you burn him?' and 'hang him up to a signpost'. Several persons secured bits of the trowsers [*sic*] in which the murderer was buried, and one regretted that he had not cut off part of his ear to preserve in spirits.

After shallowly covering the body with soil, a member of the burial party beat the earth above Steinberg's skull with an iron mallet until it was smashed to pieces.

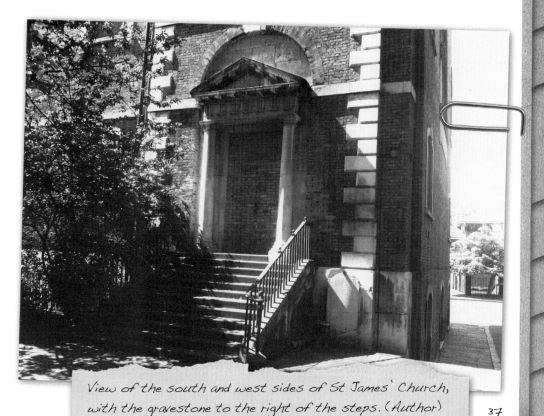

*View of the south and west sides of St James' Church, with the gravestone to the right of the steps. (Author)*

Steinberg's body was buried at night at the pauper's cemetery in Ray Street, Clerkenwell. This is a drawing of Ray Street in around 1820. (Author)

Two days later, the bodies of Ellen Lefevre and her four children were buried before a large respectful crowd at St James' Church in Clerkenwell. Agency reporters noted how 'the tops of the houses and windows, and in fact, every situation from which the burial ground could be seen, were thronged with anxious spectators of all ages and sexes'. At noon, Ellen Lefevre's mother and sister, supported by the parish beadle and a local opera singer, joined the procession of the coffins to a grave dug on the south side of the church. A public subscription paid not only for the funeral, but also for a headstone to remind everyone of the grim events at No. 17 Southampton Street. It can still be seen today at the side of the church, beside a set of stone steps leading to a doorway, although the inscription is now difficult to read.

The inscription on the gravestone begins:

Beneath this stone are deposited the remains of Ellen Lefevre, aged 25 years, and her four children - Henry, aged 5 years and 6 months.  John, aged 4 years and 6 months, Ellen, aged 2 years and 6 months, Philip, aged 8 months - Who were murdered at their residence in Southampton-street, Pentonville, during the night of the 8th September 1834, by John Nicholas Steinberg, aged 45 years, a native of Germany, and father of the above children, who afterwards murdered himself, and was buried according to law.

The inscription concludes with a poem composed by a former member of Sadler's Wells Theatre:

Poor babes could not your innocence prevail!
And when your father heard your plaintive wail
Did no compunction smite his guilty soul,
Dark thoughts of murder to control – None!
None heard your cries, in sleep the world was bound,
A gloomy death-like stillness reigned around,
While guilt with gliding footsteps noiseless trod,
You slept on earth, you woke and saw your God.
'Neath your Creator's wings in peace you're blest,
For angels wafted you to realms of rest.

At No. 17 Southampton Street, a far more gruesome memorial was being created. Less than three weeks after the murders, an unknown group of entrepreneurs rented out the house at £28 a year and turned it into a museum. The exhibition boasted a set of blood-spattered waxwork dummies laid out in the same positions in which the bodies were found, a bloody knife and visible stains on the floorboards. On the first day, the proprietors made nearly £50. So many people turned up to pay their entry fee that the 'respectable' residents of Southampton Street petitioned Hatton Garden police office to put a stop to the 'gross and indecent' spectacle. It was said that the next-door

The gravestone. (Author)

neighbours had already left the street and others were planning to do so because of the 'great injury to persons holding house property in the neighbourhood'. The magistrate refused to get involved.

There was clearly an appetite for this kind of entertainment. The following year Madame Tussaud, later famous for her 'Chamber of Horrors', established her own permanent exhibition of grisly artifacts in Baker Street.

SOLVED

Case Eight

# Who Killed Mr Templeman?

1840

Suspect:       Richard Gould

Age:           23

Charge:        Burglary

Sentence:      Transportation
               for life

In 1840, the area of Islington known as Pocock's Fields was occupied by nearly 500 people scraping an existence in small, two-roomed cottages that, to 'respectable' eyes, seemed little more than hovels. It was a poor, working-class community of bricklayers, butchers, stonemasons, drovers, rag men, dairymen, carpenters, cabinet makers and agricultural labourers. Children ran about the tiny picket-fenced gardens in bare feet, wives and mothers did the washing and cooking, or chatted to their neighbours on doorsteps, while husbands and fathers downed pitchers of ale delivered by the local public house. For residents like John Templeman, a seventy-two-year-old widower and retired damask weaver, it seemed like an ideal place to see out the last of his days; pottering about in his yard, smoking his pipe, reading religious tracts from the local church, and relaxing in his chair enjoying the view north to Holloway and the 'Highgate Archway' through his parlour window.

This peaceful scene was to be shattered on the morning of 17 March when Mr Templeman was found lying in a pool of blood on his bedroom floor, dressed only in a nightshirt. At some point during the night, burglars had broken into his cottage, prised open his chest of drawers and stolen whatever silver they could find. Then, apparently unsatisfied with their reward, they crept into his bedroom and delivered a crushing blow to the old man's temple with a wooden club, fracturing his jaw and dislodging three teeth. Somehow, Mr Templeman managed to fight his way towards the door before being overpowered. His wrists were bound together with a piece of clothesline and a stocking was tied round his head. He was then left to die. Despite the proximity of his neighbours,

The murder of John Templeman, as imagined in a drawing from 1889 in the Illustrated Police News, 23 March 1889.

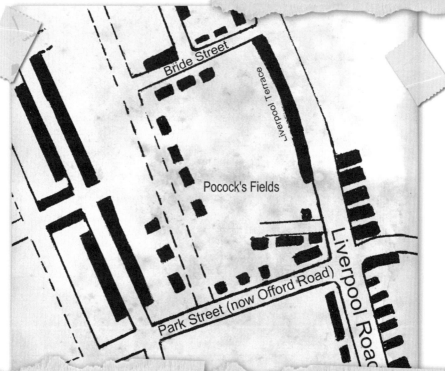

Map of Pocock's Fields in between Bridge Street and Park Street (now Offord Road). In 1840 the area to the west of Liverpool Road was still mostly open fields despite the new terraces being built near Copenhagen Road and Cloudesley Square to the south, York Place to the west and Paradise Row to the north. Within twenty years, the area was cut through by the railway and the fields became part of Arundel Square. (Author, adapted from Cary's New Plan of London, 1737)

nobody heard his cries, or the sounds of what must have been a violent struggle. It was not until eleven o'clock the next morning that the police were informed and a constable from the Islington N Division arrived to investigate.

The first thing PC William Kerr noted was that the front door was locked from the inside – whoever had murdered the old man got in via the front window by poking their finger through a hole in the glass and unfastening the button holding it shut. That crucial bit of 'local knowledge', plus the blindfolding of the victim and the manner of the killing, suggested that Mr Templeman probably knew his attackers. The motive was robbery; Mr Templeman often boasted about his wealth and had offered to buy another cottage on Pocock's Fields for £25 seven months earlier. Many of the neighbours had seen him proudly flash what appeared to be a £50 note. But Mr Templeman was merely pretending to be rich – at the time of his death he possessed approximately £6, made up of £3 in rent from one of his tenants in Somerstown and another £3 borrowed from a friend to pay off a bill. The banknote, which was found untouched in a mahogany box in the parlour, was a fake barber's voucher bearing the legend 'Bank of Elegance': 'I promise to cut or arrange any Lady or Gentleman's hair in the first style of fashion or forfeit on demand the sum of fifty pounds.'

All of which suggested that the person, or persons, responsible would be found close by. That same day the police arrested four people living within Pocock's Fields: Francis Capriani, a forty-nine-year-old nightwatchman at Sadler's Wells Theatre who did gardening work for the victim; John Jarvis and his wife Mary Ann Jarvis, close neighbours; and Richard Gould, a twenty-three-year-old former pot-boy at the nearby Barnsbury Castle pub, who had been known to take beer to the old man's door. The first of these, Capriani, was released by the magistrate the following morning – the only evidence against him was the fact that he, his wife and his mother-in-law, who were the first to see Mr Templeman lying dead in his cottage, chose to send a message to the old man's grandson in Fitzrovia rather than call the police. Capriani was, in fact, at work at the time of the murder.

Meanwhile, the gossip spread throughout Islington. On the Saturday, 'numerous respectable females' gathered in the area 'anxious to obtain a view of the cottage which has been the scene of so barbarous a murder'; two police sergeants had to guard the entrance to stop them peering inside. Newspapers compared Pocock's Fields to Nova Scotia Gardens in Bethnal Green, a location notorious as the scene of the 'Italian Boy murder' carried out by two bodysnatchers ten years earlier. Interest in the case only intensified when the three remaining suspects were hauled before the magistrate at Hatton Garden police office. As they climbed out of the police van 'all eyes were riveted upon them', reported *The Times*. 'Mrs Jarvis had her child, a fine interesting looking baby in her arms, and they were followed to the back entrance of the office by the spectators who were held back by a body of officers ... persons of great respectability flocked towards the court.' The mob reserved most of their fury for Mrs Jarvis, apparently believing that she and Gould had formed some kind of sinful bond, whereas the appearance of a dejected Mr Jarvis was greeted with 'evident sympathy'. By the end of the hearing Mr Jarvis, a hard-working painter with impeccable references, was released due to lack of evidence and given custody of the child.

The following week, Mrs Jarvis too was released after scientists discovered that the suspicious bloodstains on her apron were in fact red paint. It was not a popular decision. As Mrs Jarvis left the court with her mother she was yelled at, pelted with stones and chased up Saffron Hill into a pub on Coldbath Square. Even an escort of police officers failed to deter the crowd's thirst for vengeance and by the time they arrived at the local station in Rosoman Street, they were all covered with mud and bruises. The near-riot only ended after Mrs Jarvis and her mother were driven off at speed to a secret location in a horse-drawn cab.

Only Richard Gould would stand trial for the murder at the Old Bailey. The case against him was circumstantial, but suggested that he not only had a motive but also the opportunity to commit the crime. It was said that he was from a respectable family but had turned down the chance to emigrate to Van Diemen's Land (Tasmania) with his parents at the age of eighteen. Instead, he sought to make a life for himself in Spitalfields as a pot-boy at a public house, only to be dismissed after twelve months. Gould then enlisted as a private in the 11th Light Dragoons in Canterbury under the name of Arthur Nicholson, but soon deserted from his regiment. In late 1839, he was working at the Barnsbury Castle public house ferrying beers to the people of Pocock's Fields. It was not long before he lost this job too, and by all accounts he was virtually penniless by the time of the murder. On 12 March, he was overheard telling a friend that he knew of an old man who had been flashing a £50 note round – Gould was looking for someone to help him steal it. 'Or I could do it myself,' he added. The following night he visited John Jobson, a painter living in Dorset Street, Spitalfields, and asked for a 'screw', or a pick for a lock, and a 'darkey', or dark lantern. 'He said he was going to serve an old gentleman in a lonely cottage,' said Jobson. 'I told him if he did he would be sure to get transported. He told me he might as well, for if he was taken as a deserter he was sure to be transported anyway.'

The evening before the murder, Gould drank and played skittles at the Rainbow pub in Liverpool Road. He was last seen walking in the direction of Mr Templeman's cottage shortly before midnight, carrying a rushlight in his hand and a wooden stick in the pocket of his shooting jacket. But it was not until around two or three in the morning that he turned up at his bed in bootmaker Charles Allen's cottage on Pocock's Fields. The next day they were talking about the murder of Mr Templeman when Gould remarked that, 'if the Ten Commandments were just he had broken them all, for adultery he had committed many times, and drunkenness'. According to Mrs Allen, Gould told her 'many poor creatures like me would rather be hung than transported'. Gould also appeared to have come into some money, judging by the new shoes on his feet. Mr Allen waited for Gould to go to bed at nine o'clock in the evening before sending for Inspector James Miller of the local police.

When Gould was arrested for murder at eleven o'clock on the night of 17 March, he replied, 'If I was as innocent of everything as I am of that, I should not have much to fear.' He also dismissed the finding of bloodstains on his waistcoat, insisting this was a common occurrence given his tendency to get into fights. Further evidence emerged the next morning when a stocking containing 19 half crowns, 48s and seven sixpences was found hidden in the rafters above the privy. Coincidentally or not, this was close to the amount believed to have been in Mr Templeman's possession at the time of his death.

Inspector Miller later filed a report setting out eight reasons why he was convinced of Gould's involvement in the murder. They included his friendship with Mrs Jarvis, who lived just a few yards from the victim; the testimony of his former friends; his silence as to his movements between midnight and three in the morning; and the determined resistance of Mr Templeman which suggested there was only one robber. However, the barrister representing Gould, Mr Chambers, argued that the evidence was 'the most vague and unsatisfactory ever brought forward in support of such a charge'. The whole case was an extraordinary mystery, from the failure of Mr Templeman's neighbours to alert the police, to the suspicious testimony of Mr and Mrs Allen.

Giltspur Compter, where Richard Gould was held after his acquittal of murder in 1840. It was demolished in 1853 and replaced by a Royal Mail sorting office. The spot is now occupied by an investment bank. From Old and New London. (Author)

Having listened patiently from ten in the morning until half past eleven at night on Tuesday 14 April, the jury took only a few minutes to find Gould not guilty of murder. 'The verdict appeared to excite considerable dissatisfaction in the minds of many persons … ,' reported the *Newgate Calendar*:

> … and so great was the anger exhibited by a great portion of the populace, that the prisoner deemed it prudent to accept an offer of protection which was made to him by the sheriffs, and to remain in the Compter prison until the popular clamour should have in some degree subsided.

But the story was not over yet. A few weeks later the police were tipped off that a suitably sized reward might induce Gould to reveal the truth about the murder.

On 6 May 1840, the Home Secretary Lord Normanby announced that £100 and a pardon was available to 'any person not the actual perpetrator of the crime who gives such information and evidence as will lead to the conviction of the murderer of Mr Templeman' (a similar reward was on offer in relation to the murder of the retired MP Lord William Russell). A sergeant from the Whitehall A Division, Charles Otway, was dispatched to see Gould and obtain a confession.

Sergeant Otway arrived at the Compter to find that Gould had decided to take up the offer of free passage to Australia under the false name of Kelly. Determined to catch his man, Otway rushed to intercept the ship at Gravesend and presented Gould with an official letter detailing the terms of the reward, telling him that he could not be tried again for the murder under the law of double jeopardy. Swayed by the amount of money on offer, Gould made a statement implicating both Mr and Mrs Jarvis in the crime:

It was first proposed in consequence of him showing his notes, but it was not settled until Sunday morning, when I was at Jarvis' and then it was arranged that we should go on Monday night; and I went away early on Sunday because Jarvis expected his brother. But before I went, Jarvis got a piece of wood out of the garden which he used as a dibber. He made a hole in it, through which he put a piece of string so as to hang it on his wrist. After that I went to the Flora Tavern, York Place and got drunk. I was to have seen Jarvis early next morning but in consequence of lying in bed so late, Mrs Jarvis came down to Allen's and brought a message from Jarvis stating that I was not to go near their house till after the public houses were closed at night, but I did go with her, as she had got breakfast ready, and said there would be no fear of being noticed. I then went to the Rainbow and stopped till near 12 at night, and then went to Jarvis' being a few minutes past 12. Me and Jarvis went out together. Mrs Jarvis stopped under the portico, to watch, in case any one came she might give the alarm. I went in first, by the window and broke a bit of paper out, and a little bit of glass as well; I got my finger in and undid the button. I then got in and Jarvis got in after me. After I got in, the chisel Jarvis had brought I got from him and broke the door open. We could not find anything but the silver in a box – no sovereigns or gold there. Jarvis went into the bedroom. He said, as I could not find the notes, most likely he had them under his head. He then said 'we must make him quiet and fast'. Jarvis then struck him with the stick. The old man jumped right out of bed. Jarvis then knocked him down, and held his hands while I tied them with the clothesline we brought with us. Jarvis then tied the stocking over his eyes. We then made another search for the notes, and I found them wrapped up in some other papers in the drawer where we had found the silver in the box; we had before overlooked them. I told Jarvis they were no account, only barbers' notes, and we left them behind. The old man had then come round by this time and said 'I know you'. I jumped out of the window. Jarvis said we should be sure to be found out; he then said 'I would rather settle him than be found out' and went back into the room. He then came out of the window the same way as we got in and we went to Jarvis' house where Mrs Jarvis was outside of the door.

He claimed he had thrown the murder weapon in the New River and the dark lantern in a pond in Pocock's Fields.

Arundel Fields in Arundel Square in 2012, built on Pocock's Fields by the early 1860s. Not far to the west is Pentonville Prison, begun in 1840 and completed by 1842. (Author)

Gould's reward was not the £100 he expected, but a trip to Coldbath Fields Prison and a new trial for burglary. Mr and Mrs Jarvis were arrested for a second time only to be released again due to lack of evidence. This time Gould would defend himself at the Old Bailey, arguing that he had been tricked into making the confession by Sergeant Otway. 'Mark the time he comes, at eleven o'clock at night, when I am in bed and asleep, taking me by surprise,' he told the jury.

> He represented himself as a gentleman, sent to me by the Secretary of State, with an especial message to offer me 100 pounds if I could give him any information that would lead to the conviction of the parties concerned in the murder of Mr Templeman. I at once told him that I did not know anything about it. He then sat down, and began reasoning with me, telling me as I was a young man, and about leaving the country, how serviceable money would be to me, how much better it would be to go out with 200 pounds in my pocket than nothing at all, and as I had seen a great deal of trouble, I should be very foolish if I did not now make something of it, if I could ... I made up my mind to tell a lie for the sake of a reward ... Now, gentlemen, I will appeal to you whether, if it is not an unlawful proceeding, it is not, at least, a very unfair one?

This time the jury, after deliberating for fifteen minutes, returned a verdict of guilty. The judge sentenced him to transportation for life, remarking that, 'there could be very little doubt in the minds of all those who heard the trial that he was the person by whom the murder was perpetrated'. Gould would be sent to a penal colony 'to pass the remainder of his existence in hopeless slavery, poverty and misery of the worst description'. The audience in the public gallery clapped as Gould was led from the dock down to the cells. A month later, on 8 July 1840, Richard Gould left England on a ship to New South Wales with 270 other convicts, never to return.

# No. 39 Hilldrop Crescent

## 1910

| | |
|---|---|
| *Suspect:* | *Dr Hawley Harvey Crippen* |
| *Age:* | *48* |
| *Charge:* | *Murder* |
| *Sentence:* | *Execution* |

The couple moving into the terraced house at No. 39 were an odd match. The husband, thin, angular, his eyes bulging behind his gold-rimmed spectacles and his moustache drooping mournfully over his lips, seemed the complete opposite to his full-figured wife, who positively vibrated with energy and enthusiasm as she directed him this way and that. It was 21 September 1905, and Hawley Harvey Crippen had been married to Cora Crippen for thirteen years, a union which had taken them from Jersey City in the United States of America to a quiet, shabby but respectable crescent of semi-detached houses a few hundred metres away from Holloway Prison. The rent was £50 a year and gave them full use of the basement and another ten or so rooms on the three floors above, which were soon occupied by a menagerie of canaries, two Persian cats, a bull

*Drawing of No. 39 at the time of the murder (Author)*

terrier and the occasional lodger or two, as well as Cora's extensive wardrobe. Her collection of silk dresses, rustling underskirts, fur coats, satin gowns, and high-heeled shoes filled two bedrooms by themselves.

At first they lived quietly together, Cora doing the domestic work and cooking the meals while her husband, a homeopathic doctor, sat in his office dispensing dubious remedies, with even more questionable names like 'Special Nerve Remedy' and 'Blood Tonic'. In the evenings they played whist with the lodgers, or listened to the gramophone that Crippen had bought for his wife for Christmas. He appeared a quiet, polite and devoted husband with little taste for the usual vices of mankind, other than the occasional light ale or stout. He was not the kind to flirt, or make jokes. About the only thing that marked him out from the crowd was a slightly eccentric dress sense, but even that was dictated by his wife. They were virtually unknown to their neighbours, apart from the occasional sighting in the garden, with Cora watching on as Crippen tended to the plants. 'Peter, the rose bushes need pruning,' she would tell him, refusing to use his real name because she thought it sounded ridiculous.

Cora soon got bored of her life in the suburbs. She wanted to return to her old dream of being an entertainer, an opera singer and a music hall star, and after a series of quarrels (witnessed by one of the lodgers between December 1906 and April 1907), she persuaded her husband to pay for singing lessons. Her early performances as 'Belle Elmore' earned her a few kind reviews as 'a clever comedienne' but one of her idols, Marie Lloyd, cruelly remarked that her name on a bill would empty any theatre in the country. Eventually, she found her calling as an organiser and fundraiser for the Music Hall Ladies Guild, hustling people into buying tickets and programmes for their events. In 1908 she was elected treasurer. It was now Crippen's job to fund her glamorous public appearances by buying extravagant clothing and expensive-looking diamond jewellery, which Cora kissed and baby-talked to as if they were the children she never

Photograph of Belle Elmore, otherwise known as Cora Crippen. (LC-DIG-ggbain-05164)

had. She dyed her dark hair blonde, and turned their quiet home, now painted pink and decorated with vases, china dogs, watercolour pictures, photographs and velvet bows, into a setting for whirlwind socialising, cocktail parties and late-night soirées. Cora was also receiving the attentions of a 'one-man band' act called Bruce Miller, who sent her letters adorned with kisses.

Perhaps Crippen didn't mind his wife's newfound vigour at first – he had already begun an affair with a younger woman, his private secretary Ethel Le Neve. They had first met in 1901 at the Drouet Institute for the Deaf, where he was a thirty-nine-year-old physician and she an eighteen-year-old shorthand typist. A lonely young woman with few friends or family in London, she came to depend on Crippen's friendship, perhaps even idolising him. He listened to her problems and impressed her with talk of his expertise in valuing diamonds. An unlikely, surprisingly passionate relationship developed, with illicit meetings at hotels after work, before Crippen returned home for the night. But Le Neve wasn't happy sharing her older lover with his larger-than-life wife and sought his assurances that he would seek a divorce. Crippen, harried from all sides, was struggling with the emotional, physical and material costs of keeping two women satisfied with expensive gifts. He was overdrawn at the bank and his £600 savings would not be available for another year. Then, suddenly, at the beginning of February 1910, Cora Crippen disappeared.

She had last been seen alive on 31 January when the Crippens invited their friends Paul and Clara Martinetti to dinner at No. 39 Hilldrop Crescent. Cora prepared a plain meal of soup, a joint of beef with salad, a choice of dessert and coffee and liqueurs to finish. Crippen nursed a glass of stout throughout, while Cora indulged herself with a cigarette. Afterwards they went upstairs to play whist in the living room. 'We spent a pleasant evening and there was no quarrel of any sort,' recalled Mrs Martinetti. They left at half one in the morning. 'Mrs Crippen came to the top of the steps and wished me goodbye. She was in quite good health.'

Later that morning, Crippen arrived at work at his office in New Oxford Street as usual. The following day, according to Le Neve, he told her that his wife had gone to America. 'I found her gone when I got home last night,' she remembered him saying. 'She always said that the things I gave her were not good enough, so I suppose she thinks she can get better elsewhere.' Crippen gave her some of his wife's jewellery, including a small diamond brooch designed to resemble the rising sun. The rest he pawned for £175 at a shop just down the road from his workplace. Crippen also got Le Neve to take a letter to the committee of the Music Hall Ladies Guild. It purported to come from Belle Elmore, but was not in her writing:

> Please forgive me a hasty letter and any inconvenience I may cause you, but I have just had news of the illness of a near relative, and at only a few hours' notice I am obliged to go to America. Under the circumstances I cannot return for several months, and I therefore beg you to accept this as a formal resignation from this date of the honorary treasurership ... I ask my good friends and pals to accept my sincere and loving wishes for their own personal welfare. Believe me, yours faithfully, Belle Elmore.

Three weeks later, Crippen made his first public appearance with Le Neve at the Music Hall Benevolent Fund Dinner and Ball. To the dismay of Cora's friends, Le Neve was wearing the diamond 'rising sun' brooch openly, as if trying to emulate Mrs Crippen, or perhaps replace her entirely. Le Neve also proudly showed off a diamond solitaire ring, claiming that it was her engagement ring, and started giving her friends any of Cora's belongings that she did not want for herself – coats, feather boas, blouses, skirts, stockings, shoes, hats and even nightgowns. On 12 March she moved out of her flat permanently and into Crippen's bed.

The following week Crippen sent a letter to his friends the Martinettis saying that his wife was dangerously ill with pneumonia, shortly followed by a telegram announcing that Belle had passed away. He placed a short death notice in the *Era* newspaper: 'ELMORE – March 23, in California, USA, Miss Belle Elmore (Mrs H.H. Crippen).'

The news came as a shock to her friends at the guild, but they were unable to ask Crippen more about it because he and Le Neve had already left for a week's holiday across the Channel in Dieppe. When they finally managed to see him at his office, Crippen told them that there was no need for them to contact Belle's friends or family in America and that her ashes would be sent over to England.

It was past Easter when he found the time to send a letter to Cora's sister, then living in New York:

> I hardly know how to write to you my dreadful loss. The shock to me has been so dreadful that I am hardly able to control myself. My poor Cora has gone, and to make the shock to me more dreadful I did not even see her

at the last. A few weeks ago we had news that an old relative of mine in California was dying, and to secure important property for ourselves it was necessary for one of us to go and put the matter in the lawyer's hands at once. As I was very busy, Cora proposed she should go, and, as it was necessary for someone to go there at once, she would go straight through from here to California without stopping at all, and then return by way of Brooklyn, when she would pay all of you a long visit. Unfortunately, on the way out my poor Cora caught a severe cold, and, not having a chance to take proper care of herself while travelling, it settled on her lungs, and later developed into pleuro-pneumonia. She wished not to frighten me, and said it was a slight matter, and the next I heard was she was dangerously ill, and two days later, after I had cabled to know should I go to her, the dreadful news came that she had passed away. Imagine, if you can, the dreadful shock to me; never more to see my Cora alive, nor hear her voice again. She is being sent back to me, and I shall soon have what is left of her here. Of course, I am giving up the house. In fact, it drives me mad to be in it alone. I don't know what I shall do; probably find some business to take me travelling for a few months until I can recover from the shock a little. It is so terrible to me to have to write this dreadful news. Will you please tell the others of our loss? Love to all …

Meanwhile the ladies of the Music Hall Guild pursued their suspicions about the disappearance of Belle Elmore, even going to the trouble of writing to Crippen's son in Los Angeles to seek confirmation. On 30 June, John Nash, the husband of music hall entertainer Lil Hawthorne, went to the police.

The investigation was handed to Chief Inspector Walter Dew, a forty-seven-year-old detective who had served in the Whitechapel Division at the time of the Jack the Ripper murders. His investigation proceeded at a leisurely pace, and it was not until the morning of 8 July that he saw Crippen at his office in Oxford Street. Almost immediately, Crippen confessed that he had completely fabricated the story of his wife's death. 'As far as I know she is still alive,' he added, claiming that she had announced that she was leaving him during a row after dinner with the Martinettis. Crippen agreed to show Inspector Dew around No. 39 Hilldrop Crescent and suggested that he should place an advertisement in the newspapers in an attempt to locate his wife. Impressed by Crippen's cool, unflustered demeanour, and seeing nothing suspicious at the house, Inspector Dew left to continue his enquiries. The next day Crippen and Le Neve fled the country.

The disguises were Crippen's idea. He shaved off his moustache, while Le Neve cut her hair short and dressed up as a boy in a brown tweed suit, shirt, collar and tie, braces, black boots and a bowler hat. The final touch was a cigarette dangling from her lips. 'You will do famously,' he told her on completing the costume. 'No one will recognise you. You are a perfect boy!' Crippen appeared to be enjoying himself immensely as they set off by tube to Liverpool Street, exhilarated by the success of the deception and the novelty of having a 'pretty boy' as a companion. Even the realisation that they had missed the train did not dampen his enthusiasm. They spent the three-hour wait taking a tour of Hackney by bus, before catching the train to Harwich and the night boat to Holland. On 9 July they booked into a hotel in Brussels, secure in their new identities of John Robinson, a fifty-five-year-old merchant from Quebec, and his sixteen-year-old deaf and mute son.

Back in England, the oblivious Chief Inspector Dew circulated a description of Cora Crippen as a missing person. It was another two days before he discovered that Crippen had also disappeared. This time he carried out a thorough search of No. 39 Hilldrop Crescent and uncovered a loaded revolver in a wardrobe in the front bedroom on the first floor, together with a box containing forty-five bullets. He established the circumstances of their flight, circulated their descriptions at the ports and began digging up the garden. Then on 13 July, Dew examined the cellar:

It had a brick floor. I probed about with a poker; at one place I found that the poker went rather easily in between the crevices and I got a few bricks up. I then got a spade and dug the clay immediately beneath the bricks. About nine inches below, I came across what appeared to be human remains.

It was not a recognisable body. There was no skeleton, no head, no limbs or genitals, merely a lumpy puddle of skin, flesh and internal organs. Identifying a gender was impossible, although several items suggested that it was a woman – a section of a cotton undervest, a hair curler, and part of a pyjama jacket bearing the label of a shirt maker from Holloway. Whoever had buried the remains had added lime in a failed attempt to destroy them – the lime was wet and had in fact preserved the heart, lungs, liver, kidneys, spleen, stomach and pancreas in perfect condition. One thing was certain – this was now a murder enquiry, as well as a sensational newspaper story.

The *Islington Gazette* led the way with a description of the scene, now thronged with 'the usual morbid crowd', under the headline, 'The Green Crescent of the Crime':

> Hilldrop Crescent is a quiet suburban place although in the inner ring of the metropolis; and reasoning superficially, it would be the last spot one would have dreamt of for the stage of a sordid murder. The exterior aspect of the quiet residential streets speaks of respectability; and in the placid atmosphere of well-to-do Suburbia the tokens of the grim deed seized the heart with a greater shock than they would have done in the denser and darker neighbourhood that lies not far away.

Reporters now swarmed about the area asking neighbours, shopkeepers and local busybodies for juicy gossip. Lena Lyons, whose garden at No. 46 Brecknock Road backed on to the Crippen house, claimed to have heard two shots one morning in January or February. Another resident heard a scream, 'which terminated with a long dragging whine' but dismissed it as the screech of a prostitute plying her trade in nearby Parmetes Row. Louisa Glackner thought she heard cries of 'Oh don't, oh don't' coming from the direction of No. 39 Hilldrop. There were also dim memories of the burning of rubbish in the garden at around the time of Cora's disappearance.

While detectives scrambled to trace their prime suspect, Crippen and Le Neve spent a leisurely ten days sightseeing in Brussels before making their way to Antwerp. On 20 July, they boarded the SS *Montrose* and set off across the Atlantic Ocean for Quebec.

John Robinson and his son soon attracted the attention of the ship's captain, Commander Henry George Kendall. They had no baggage and stood out among the mainly non-English immigrants hoping to start a new life in the New World. 'We had taken a second-class cabin, which was quite cosy, and to me the whole ship was wonderful,' remembered Le Neve.

> I found plenty to amuse me, for Captain Kendall supplied me with plenty of literature in the shape of novels and magazines, not forgetting some detective stories. I spent many hours on deck with Dr Crippen, but naturally I kept rather aloof from the other passengers and did not speak very much. On the other hand, when any of the officers spoke to me I did not hesitate to reply and did not feel

in the least embarrassed. I felt so sure of myself. I remember there was one nice English boy with whom I got rather chummy. We used to talk football together!

Dr Crippen spent most of his time reading Dickens' *The Pickwick Papers*.

Unbeknownst to the fugitives, Captain Kendall had already used a relatively new invention to alert Scotland Yard about his suspicious passengers – the wireless telegraph. As the ship passed 130 miles west of Cornwall, he sent the message: 'Have strong suspicion that Crippen London Cellar murderer and accomplice are amongst saloon passengers. Moustache shaved off, growing beard. Accomplice dressed as boy, voice, manner and build undoubtedly a girl.' This crucial tip-off allowed Chief Inspector Dew to race to Liverpool to catch a faster ship to Quebec, the *Laurentic*, on 23 July. Eight days later, after boarding the SS *Montrose* at Father Point, Dew had his prey brought up to the captain's cabin.

'Good morning Dr Crippen,' he said.

'Good morning,' replied Crippen calmly, apparently unsurprised at this turn of events. After being informed that he would be arrested for the murder and mutilation of his wife, one of his first thoughts appears to have been for Le Neve. 'It is only fair to say she knows nothing about it. I never told her anything.' He is also said to have blurted out: 'I am not sorry; the anxiety has been too much.' At all other times he remained polite, even cheerful, and happy to indulge in small talk with the police officers watching his every move as he was taken first to Quebec and then back across the ocean to Liverpool. On 27 August, Dew was able to parade his prisoners in triumph before a large crowd eager to see the monster that they had read about almost every day for the last two months.

Back in England, the detectives and medical experts had been busy trying to prove that the remains in the cellar belonged to Cora Crippen and to establish a solid case against the now notorious Dr Crippen. At the beginning of August, detectives discovered that on 19 January Crippen had visited a chemist's shop in Oxford Street to collect

Dr Crippen and Le Neve appear in the dock at Bow Street Magistrates' Court before their trial at the Old Bailey. (LC-DIG-ggbain-08612)

a batch of the sedative hyoscine, which if taken in large enough doses could cause loss of consciousness, paralysis and death. Alerted to the find, Dr William Willcox, the 'senior scientific analyst to the Home Office', examined the internal organs recovered from No. 39 Hilldrop Crescent and was able to detect traces of the same drug. Augustus Pepper, a consultant surgeon at St Mary's Hospital, concluded that it was 'quite impossible' that the body parts had been buried in the cellar before Mr and Mrs Crippen moved there in September 1905. The internal organs had been removed from the body intact and were still connected to each other, demonstrating that the person responsible knew at least how to dissect an animal. 'From the remains I examined I should say that the person in life was an adult, young or middle aged, and of stout figure.'

The crucial piece of evidence turned out to be a 4in-long mark found on one of the pieces of skin. Mrs Martinetti had told detectives that she saw 'an old cut' on the stomach of Cora Crippen the previous summer. Informed of this evidence, a young pathologist called Dr Bernard Spilsbury examined the skin under a microscope and concluded: 'The mark is undoubtedly an old operation scar.' Dr Spilsbury would go on to give a convincing performance at the Old Bailey trial in October 1910 – the first step in his career as a 'celebrity pathologist' and the 'father of forensic medicine'.

Crippen was forty-eight years old when he entered the witness box in an attempt to clear his name. He told the story of a cuckolded husband, mistreated by his hot-headed wife and forced to seek solace in the arms of his devoted secretary. The marriage to Cora had become a sham – they may have kept up the pretence in front of their friends but at home they slept in separate rooms and quarrelled endlessly over trivial things. As for the fateful evening of 31 January, he had again been the victim of her foul temper. 'While they were there she picked a quarrel with me upon a most trivial incident,' he told the court.

During the evening Mr Martinetti wanted to go upstairs. As he had been to the house many times and knew the place perfectly well, I let him go up by himself. When he came down he seemed to have caught a chill. When the Martinettis had left, my wife got into a great rage about this. She abused me, and said some very strong things. She said that if I could not be a gentleman she had had enough of it and could not stand it any longer and she was going to leave. I came back the next day at my usual time, which would be about half-past seven or eight o'clock, and found that the house was vacant.

Believing she had had gone to Chicago to join Bruce Miller, he sought to cover up his shame with lies. As for his flight from London, he thought the suspicion was so great that he would be kept in prison for months until his wife was found. 'The only idea I could think of was to take Le Neve away out of the country, where she would not have this scandal thrown upon her.' Crippen made sure to exonerate his lover of any possible responsibility.

His barrister, Edward Marshall Hall, called his own medical evidence to cast doubt on the testimony of Spilsbury, Willcox and Pepper – it was claimed the 'scar' was simply a fold of skin – but the jury were not persuaded. They took just twenty-seven minutes to find Crippen guilty. Asked if he wanted to say anything, he replied: 'I still protest my innocence.'

Crippen was not short of supporters – more than 15,000 people signed a petition calling for him to be spared the death sentence. Women seemed particularly sympathetic to his situation, a henpecked husband whose only thought was for the well-being of his true love, Ethel Le Neve. This remained true right up to his execution at Pentonville Prison on 23 November; it was at least some comfort for him that Le Neve was acquitted of being an accessory after the fact. His final letter, printed in a newspaper three days before his death, read:

**ETHEL LE NEVE**

*HER LIFE STORY*

With the True Account of Their Flight and Her Friendship for

**DR. CRIPPEN**

TOLD BY HERSELF

*Ethel C Le Neve*

COPYRIGHT

Front cover of Ethel Le Neve, Her Life Story, with the true account of their flight and her friendship for Dr Crippen, told by herself. (Author)

> I solemnly state that I knew nothing of the remains discovered at Hilldrop Crescent until I was told of their discovery by my solicitor … I desire the world to have pity on a woman who, however weak she may have seemed in their eyes, has been loyal in the midst of misery and to the very end of tragedy, and whose love has been self-sacrificing and strong.

Despite the strong circumstantial evidence, there remains some doubt as to whether Crippen did in fact murder his wife. In 2007, a forensic scientist from Michigan State University claimed that DNA testing on the 100-year-old tissue samples revealed they were in fact male and did not match the descendants of Cora Crippen. If this is the case, it would imply Crippen killed someone else. But there is still the problem of the missing wife – is it possible that Cora started a new life without contacting any of her friends or relatives, or died elsewhere, unknown and unrecognised? And what happened to the rest of the body? Did Crippen burn it in the kitchen grate, as stated in a supposed confession printed in the *Evening Times,* or did he throw it overboard during his trip to Dieppe? Why did he bury the skin and organs in his cellar? It is a strange mixture of evil cunning and blundering incompetence, a fiendish plan that never quite worked as intended.

As for No. 39 Hilldrop Crescent, its reputation as a cursed 'House of Horrors' lingered for another thirty years. Crippen's furniture was sold off before the trial started, but raised less than £150 – including £14 for the 'cottage piano' that Cora Crippen sang along to when practising her act. There were apocryphal tales of shrieks and scraping noises coming from the house on winter nights. Its reputation put off many new tenants until a fifty-year-old Scottish comedian and 'music hall artiste' took up the lease on the cheap. His name was Adam Arthur but he performed as 'Sandy McNab', regularly touring the country with his act 'The Egyptian Mummy.' He was living at No. 39 by January 1911, when he put an advert in *The Stage*: 'In a new version of Scotch Sketch "King Pharaoh" drawing record houses everywhere. Resting by doctor's orders. Many thanks to all for the many letters and wires wishing speedy recovery.' He is also recorded in the 1911 census as living at No. 39 with his wife, Bessie, forty-one, son, Willie, twenty-two, and daughter, Maud, eighteen. Later that year he set off on a tour of South Africa.

Sandy McNab standing at the doorway of No. 39 Hilldrop Crescent in 1911. (National Archives)

In 1912, back in England, he continued to happily advertise the fact that he was living in Crippen's old house. In April, the *Western Times* reported:

An exciting python hunt has taken place at 39 Hilldrop Crescent, the house formerly occupied by Crippen. The python belongs to Mr Sandy McNab, the music hall artist, and only reached England from South Africa on Friday. It celebrated its arrival by breaking out of its cage the first night, and awakened Mr McNab by a terrific smash of crockery. Mr McNab said he found it after a long search, coiled up on a shelf under the hot water tank.

Then in August he appeared in *The Times* newspaper under the headline 'Highway Robbery in North London':

Mr Sandy McNab, a comedian, who occupies the house in Hilldrop-Crescent, formerly tenanted by Crippen, was knocked down outside his house early yesterday morning and robbed of a gold medal presented to him by the South African Amalgamated Theatres Limited. Mr McNab offers £50 reward for the recovery of the medal. It is the size of a five shilling piece, slightly oval in form and studded with 16 diamonds. Engraved on the medal is the inscription: 'presented to Sandy McNab by the South African Amalgamated Theatres, January 1912.'

In his book *Crippen: The Mild Murderer*, the journalist Tom Cullen claimed that McNab's lease was terminated after neighbours objected to his plans to turn the house into a 'Crippen Museum'. This may be yet another Islington myth – a more likely explanation is that the house fell empty when Sandy McNab was sentenced to two years' hard labour in June 1914 for seducing a thirteen-year-old girl who hoped that he would help her get into show business.

The curse of No. 39 Hilldrop Crescent struck for the last time on 8 September 1940 when a German bomb demolished the rear wall. Together with the adjoining No. 40, it was torn down and eventually replaced with a four-storey block of flats. The new building was named after Britain's first female Cabinet minister, Margaret Bondfield, and remains there to this day.

SOLVED

# No. 63 Tollington Park

## 1911

Suspect:       Frederick Seddon

Age:            40

Charge:        Murder by Poisoning

Sentence:      Execution

Shortly after midnight the cry of a woman echoed out from the top-floor window: 'I'm dying.' The voice belonged to Eliza Barrow, a forty-nine-year-old partially deaf spinster lying helpless upon a bed stained with vomit and diarrhoea. Hordes of fat, black flies buzzed randomly about the room, gliding on the warm, fetid air rising from the sheets. The foul smell easily overpowered the antiseptic fumes emanating from carbolic-acid-soaked sheets hanging by the doorway, which was noticeable throughout the entire house. Ms Barrow had been like this for two weeks, rolling about the soiled mattress, clutching her stomach in pain and complaining of chills in her feet. Morphine only briefly dulled the sharp ache in her belly and the bismuth prescribed by the doctor did little to restrain her bowel movements. But it was not long – only six hours – until she found peace in death while her killer watched coolly from the bedroom doorway.

The setting for the murder of Eliza Barrow was No. 63 Tollington Park in Upper Holloway. A journalist later described Tollington Park as 'a road with pretentions to more than mere respectability'. The houses suggest not what buildings of similar capacity in other districts so often suggest – a decayed and fallen gentility – but rather a crescent and gratified prosperity. You feel that the people who live there have come not from a better neighbourhood, but from one not so good, and that they are proud to live in Tollington Park.

Frederick Seddon bought the house at No. 63 as an investment rather than as a family home. His original plan was to rent it out as flats, but in January 1910 he changed his mind. With fourteen rooms over four storeys there was more than enough space for his wife, father, five children and the servant, meaning that he could rent out the whole of the top floor as a flat at 12s 6d a week. To maximise his earnings further, he set up his office in the basement and charged 5s a week in rent to his employers, the London and Manchester Industrial Assurance Co. He even extracted 6s a week from his sons for board and lodging.

The house at No. 63 Tollington Park, scene of the murder of Eliza Barrow on 14 September 1911. (Author)

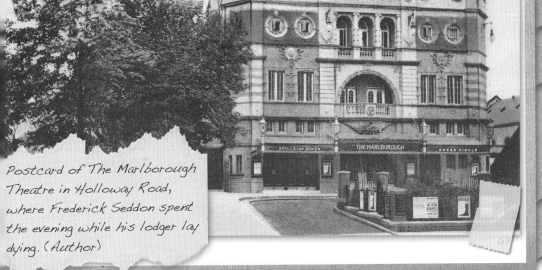

Postcard of The Marlborough Theatre in Holloway Road, where Frederick Seddon spent the evening while his lodger lay dying. (Author)

This insatiable hunger for money – or even better, solid gold– affected Frederick Seddon's whole life. He entered the insurance business at the age of nineteen and became district superintendent at twenty-six. He boasted that he had sold his first property for a profit of more than £400 and had gone on to acquire seventeen other properties in addition to Tollington Park. His conversation was dominated by money and the famously rich, and his wit extended to bemoaning his ill fortune in having no rich aunt or uncle to leave him a fortune. He was in the habit of carrying around £50 in his pockets, possibly just so he could impress his friends and acquaintances, and always kept between £100 and £200 in gold sovereigns in his safe, 'in order to pick up any cheap stocks for cash'. In fact, Seddon had two safes – one in his basement office and one in his bedroom, so that he could more easily count his money like an Edwardian Scrooge.

By the autumn of 1911, Seddon was forty years old and moving relentlessly up in the world, while his thirty-four-year-old wife, Margaret, dutifully reared their offspring. She had only given birth to the youngest, a baby girl called Lily, that January, but Frederick wasn't about to waste money on more servants – she continued to do the housework and look after the lodgers with the help of one maid and a part-time charwoman. If she resented her husband's authoritarian attitude, she was either unwilling or too afraid to show it.

On 13 September, Frederick Seddon left his wife at home while he enjoyed the evening at the Marlborough Theatre, No. 383 Holloway Road, which was, that week, staging a performance of *The Whip*, a melodramatic play featuring a real-life horse race on stage, a train crash and a mock-up of Madame Tussaud's Chamber of Horrors.

Any other man might have found himself entertained and amused, but Seddon spent the entire performance brooding over a dispute with the cashier, who had mistakenly given him change for a florin instead of half a crown. Frederick Seddon wasn't the kind to suffer the loss of 6d in silence, so he made sure his wife had to suffer as well by griping about it at length on his return home. When he was told that Ms Barrow claimed she was dying, he asked his wife, 'Is she?'

Mrs Seddon smiled and replied, 'No.' While she attempted to relieve Ms Barrow's suffering with hot flannels, Seddon appeared annoyed by the inconvenience.

When Ms Barrow asked for brandy he was unable to restrain himself from exclaiming, 'My good woman, don't you know it is after one o'clock in the morning? We can't get brandy now.'

Mrs Seddon, a little more sympathetic to her plight, checked the bottle and found that there was a swig left which could be mixed with soda. It was gone two when they returned downstairs to sleep.

They hadn't been in bed long when Ernie Grant, a ten-year-old orphan boy living with Ms Barrow, knocked on the door to say that Chickie, as he called her, had got out of bed and was bent double in pain on the floor. Ernie recalled:

Eliza Barrow, who died at the age of forty-nine. (Author)

> She sent me down for Mrs Seddon more than twice that night ... I cannot remember how many times. She only told me to go down and call her as she felt so ill. She told me to tell her that she had pains in her stomach. During that part of the night she was badly sick more than once. She got out of bed and sat on the floor. She said 'I am going' – she seemed in great pain.

Ernie, who slept in the same bed as Ms Barrow, claimed not to notice any 'nasty smell' but perhaps he was just being polite. 'She was always an affectionate and loving woman to me,' he said.

After yet another bout of sickness at around four o'clock in the morning, Mrs Seddon decided to stay at the bedside in a basket chair, while Mr Seddon remained at the door smoking and reading. Eventually, Ms Barrow fell asleep. 'She was snoring for an hour or an hour and a half after that – a kind of breathing through the mouth. My wife was dozing when this snoring did not seem quite so heavy and all of a sudden it stopped.' Seddon woke up his wife and told her, 'Good God, she's dead.'

The body of Ms Barrow had barely gone cold when Frederick Seddon set about obtaining the death certificate and arranging the funeral. He had got the first by eight o'clock in the morning – the doctor didn't even bother to see the body before signing off the cause of death as 'epidemic diarrhoea and exhaustion'. For the funeral he needed money, and he wasn't about to waste his own. And so, when he returned to Tollington Park, he began rooting through Ms Barrow's belongings. Seddon would later claim that he was only able to find £4 10s in a brown paper bag in her trunk, two silver watches, brooches, a bracelet and some clothing. By half eleven that morning, he was haggling with the undertaker at No. 78 Stroud Green Road for the cheapest funeral possible, finally agreeing a figure of £3 7s 6d, meaning he could cover the other expenses with the remaining money. Two days later, Ms Barrow was buried in a public grave in Finchley.

The story of Eliza Barrow might have ended there had it not been for her cousin Frank Vonderahe, who lived a few streets north in Corbyn Street. Unaware that she was now six feet under, he and his wife called at No. 63 Tollington Park on 20 September. The servant girl, Mary Chater, responded to his request to see Ms Barrow with startled surprise. 'Don't you know she is dead and buried?'

'No, when did she die?' replied Vonderahe.

'Last Saturday, but if you will call about nine o'clock, you will be able to see Mr Seddon and he will tell you all about it.' Yet when they returned at the requested time Seddon was not available. Mr Vonderahe's wife, Julia, managed to speak to him briefly the next day, but came away with little more than a copy of the will and a memorial card. Seddon even dared to tell her he had 'wasted enough time' on the matter and that he would not be able to speak to them again for another two weeks. He and his family were off for a pleasant seaside holiday in Southend.

When Mr Vonderahe finally managed to catch up with him on 9 October, Seddon was dismissive. 'I do not know why I should give you any information. You are not the eldest of the family.' Further questioning revealed that the majority of Ms Barrow's fortune – valued at around £4,000 – had been signed over to Seddon. In October 1910 he had persuaded her to give him her India stock, valued at £1,600, in return for an annuity of £103 for the rest of her life. Three months later he sold the stock and bought the leases on fourteen houses in Stepney. He also negotiated with Ms Barrow to buy a property she owned in Camden (the Buck's Head pub and the shop next door) in return for a further annuity of £52, in addition to staying at Tollington Park rent free. When Ms Barrow fell ill in September 1911 he persuaded her to make a will naming Seddon as the executor and Ernie Grant as the beneficiary.

Seddon almost bragged about his acquisition of Ms Barrow's assets, telling her cousin, 'I am always open to buy property. This house I live in, fourteen rooms, is my own, and I have seventeen other properties. I am always open to buy property at a price.' He confirmed the position in a formal letter sent to the Vonderahes: 'She stated in writing that she did not wish any of her relatives to receive any benefit at her death. She had simply left furniture, jewellery, and clothing. F.H. Seddon, Executor.' And when asked why Ms Barrow had been buried in a public grave instead of the family vault in Highgate, Seddon replied, 'I thought it was full up.'

Frustrated by Seddon's attitude, Frank Vonderahe went to the police with his suspicions. Five weeks later, on 14 November, Eliza Barrow's body was exhumed and sent to the pathologist William Willcox for a post-mortem. The doctor's findings, together with the expert opinion of the pathologist Bernard Spilsbury, were devastating for Seddon – Ms Barrow had been poisoned with arsenic. According to Willcox, the fatal dose was probably taken within two days of death. 'The symptoms are of a very acute and pronounced character,' he said. 'The patient is faint, collapsed, has severe pain in the abdomen, vomiting and purging; sometimes cramp in the legs; death resulting in a few days.'

On 4 December, Seddon was approached in the street in Tollington Park and arrested on suspicion of murder. Seddon's reply was curiously melodramatic:

Absurd. What a terrible charge … wilful murder. It is the first of our family that has ever been accused of such a crime. Are you going to arrest my wife as well? If not, I would like you to give her a message for me. Have they found arsenic in her body? She has not done this, herself – it was not carbolic acid was it, as there was some in her room, and Sanitas is not poison is it?

A month later his wife was also charged. Her reply was more subdued: 'Yes, very well.'

Further evidence emerged which deepened the suspicion against the Seddons; a search of No. 63 Tollington Park uncovered a watch and a ring belonging to Ms Barrow in the Seddons' wardrobe. It turned out that Frederick Seddon had commissioned a jeweller to remove Ms Barrow's name from the back of the watch and to enlarge the ring the day after her death. The Seddons claimed that they were given the jewellery as a present, but they were unable to explain what had happened to the large sum of

Valentine's Preparation Meat-Juice has a long record of successful use by the medical profession. This concentrated beef extract is readily tolerated by invalids and convalescents, even by those who cannot retain solid foods, and is accepted by children and the aged.

Valentine's Meat - Juice is an aqueous extract of lean beef, concentrated, clarified and mixed with glycerin (9% by volume). It is pleasant in flavor, and free from added seasoning. It contains meat bases, with some soluble protein derivatives, chiefly peptone and proteoses; and inorganic salts, largely the phosphates and chlorides of potassium and sodium. The Potassium content is 1000 to 1300 milli equivalents per litre (equivalent to 74-97 mg. KCl per cc.)

The Juice is essentially unaffected by temperature changes and is suitable for use in any climate, anywhere, anytime.

### USES

Valentine's Meat-Juice is especially useful when given as a fat-free broth. It stimulates the appetite and increases the flow of digestive fluids in the stomach; lessens nausea; supplies potassium in a palatable oral form for the adjunct treatment of diabetic acidosis, infant diarrheas, or wherever oral administration of potassium is indicated.

### DOSAGE AND ADMINISTRATION

Adults: One teaspoonful, two or three times daily, before meals, given in two or three tablespoonfuls of hot or cold water or the patient's favorite beverage, or poured over crushed ice. Where indicated in potassium therapy, the physician may prescribe considerably larger doses.

Children: One-half to one-third the adult dose, according to age, or as the physician may direct.

FOR USE AS A BROTH

*Advert for Valentine's Meat Juice. (Author)*

money, estimated at between £380 and £750, which Ms Barrow kept in her cash box. The only possible conclusion was that it had vanished into the Seddons' pockets. Even more damning was the evidence of a pharmacist in Crouch Hill who claimed to have sold a 3d packet of 'Mather's Arsenical flypapers, to poison flies, wasps, ants, mosquitos, etc.' to the Seddons' sixteen-year-old daughter, Maggie, on 26 August – six days before Ms Barrow was taken ill. Mrs Seddon also admitted to buying flypapers on around 4 September – but neither Ernie Grant nor the maid had noticed them being used in the house. Tests carried out by Dr Willcox showed that the arsenic could be extracted by soaking or boiling them in water. It might then have been added to the Valentine's Meat Juice that Mrs Seddon fed to Ms Barrow during her illness. 'I think arsenic might be administered in Valentine's Meat Juice without detection,' concluded Dr Willcox. 'The Valentine's Meat Juice and the fly paper solution are exactly similar in colour.'

But who had actually poisoned Ms Barrow? Frederick Seddon had motive aplenty, but there was nothing that actually put the arsenic in his hands. When the case came to trial at the Old Bailey his barrister, the legendary Edward Marshall Hall, told the jury:

You may have suspicion. You may feel that here there is a strong motive against the male prisoner. You may feel that he has behaved badly in the unfortunate matter of the funeral. You may feel many things which are to his prejudice; but I submit to you that there is no evidence whatever upon which you can find him guilty of the administration of the poison.

Unfortunately for the defence case, Frederick Seddon had insisted on entering the witness box, displaying the arrogance and supreme greed that would convince the jury of his guilt. Seddon even implied that Eliza Barrow might have mistakenly drunk the flypaper water herself to quench the thirst brought on by her illness. The jury took an hour to convict him of murder. His wife was found not guilty.

Even now, Seddon refused to be beaten. He crossed the dock to his wife and gave her a loud kiss which echoed through the silence of the court. He then took some papers out of his pocket and made a long speech insisting upon his innocence. 'Had Miss Barrow thrown herself out through the window … I would have been believed to have thrown her out or pushed her out through the window. Had Miss Barrow fallen downstairs the same thing would have applied.' In a final gamble he openly made a Masonic sign with his hand, imploring the judge to be merciful. 'I declare before the Great Architect of the Universe I am not guilty, my Lord.'

The judge, Mr Justice Bucknill, was indeed a Freemason and appeared to be overcome with emotion as he passed the death sentence:

From what you have said, you and I know we both belong to one Brotherhood and it is all the more painful to me to have to say what I am saying. But our Brotherhood does not encourage crime; on the contrary it condemns it. I pray you again to make your peace with the Great Architect of the Universe.

On 16 April 1912, two days before his execution at Pentonville Prison, he wrote a final letter to his wife:

I am still cheerful, and will be till the last, thanks to a clear conscience which sustains me, and this brings me to another important matter I wish to prepare you against. You remember in Crippen's case how false reports went about, and how he was supposed to have made a confession of his guilt; if you should see anything in the papers which you know is not true, instantly deny it … I have nothing to confess …

Illicitly taken photograph of Frederick Seddon being sentenced to death.
(Public domain, Wikipedia)

Ironically, Margaret Seddon ended up telling the *Weekly Dispatch* that she saw her husband give the poison to Ms Barrow on the night of her death.

Frederick Seddon ended his letter by trying to cast himself as the victim of the unlucky number 13. He claimed there were 13 months between Ms Barrow moving into Tollington Park and her death, 13 days between her taking ill and her death, and 13 weeks between his arrest and trial. He added:

This will be considered by many people as a mere chapter of coincidences, and I would add that the set of circumstances that has surrounded my case, which has been the means of my conviction, are just as strange, and are a mere chapter of coincidences on which a perfectly innocent or business interpretation could have been placed, but on which the prosecution placed the worst possible construction, and thus secured my conviction. There it is. Strange but true. Now I must close with sincere love and best wishes. God bless you all. Love to father. Your affectionate and innocent husband, Fred.

# No. 14 Bismarck Road

1914

Suspect: George Joseph Smith

Age: 42

Charge: Multiple Murders by Drowning

Sentence: Execution

In the middle of the First World War, the Islington street known as Bismarck Road was wiped off the map forever. This destruction was not achieved by an enemy bomb dropped from a Zeppelin (as happened in Stoke Newington, Farringdon Road and other areas of London), but as a result of the anti-German feeling sweeping the country. The animosity and threat of violence was so great that people with German-sounding names changed them to more English-sounding ones, and King George V rebranded the monarchy from Saxe-Coburg and Gotha to Windsor. Bismarck Road, built in the 1880s and named after the famous Prussian chancellor who unified Germany in 1871, was one of many street names that disappeared not only in London and across the UK, but also in Canada, the United States and Australia. 'The dislike of everything German is manifestly deepening,' it was reported in June 1916.

Not merely have residents in this country who bear names suggesting Teutonic origin taken legal steps to adopt British names, but local authorities are being bombarded with applications for the rechristening of thoroughfares called after German cities and celebrities. Even Bismarck Road is not acceptable to the inhabitants of Highgate and the Council has agreed that it shall henceforth be known as Waterlow Road.

This rechristening, using the surname of the former Liberal MP for Islington, David Sydney Waterlow, was approved by the London County Council a few months later.

But that is not the whole story. It was originally proposed that Bismarck Road should be named after Edith Cavell, the nurse whose heroism in helping Allied soldiers in occupied Brussels led to her being shot by the Germans on 12 October 1915. According

The house at No. 14 Waterlow Road, on the left with the wooden door. The murder of Margaret Lofty took place in the bathroom on the first floor. (Author

to *The Times*: 'the name Cavell was objected to on the ground that the road had obtained notoriety by a sensational murder trial.'

The murder in question had taken place a year earlier. At five o'clock on the evening of Thursday 17 December 1914, a newly-wed couple turned up on the doorstep of No. 14 Bismarck Road looking to rent a room. John and Margaret Lloyd were a little flustered, after having been turned away from another house in Orchard Road, half a mile north, and forced to search for an alternative lodging through the cold, dark streets of Highgate. The landlady took them up to a furnished bedroom on the second floor and told them it would cost 7s a week. As they came back down the stairs Mrs Lloyd asked: 'Have you got a bath?'

Yes, they did, replied Miss Blatch, pointing to the bathroom on the first floor. After paying the first week's bill, the husband went to fetch the luggage they had left at the train station. When he returned they went out for the evening, before returning for their first night together as a married couple.

John Lloyd, who claimed to be a thirty-eight-year-old land agent, was clearly the dominant figure in the marriage and had a habit of answering any questions directed at his wife before she could answer. He had an aura about him, a magnetic gaze that, together with the well-tended moustache, spoke of authority. By contrast his wife Margaret, also thirty-eight, was introverted, quiet and serious, perhaps even a little dowdy. Still, they seemed happy enough together the following morning, despite Mr Lloyd's claims that his wife had not been feeling well. 'She is better,' he told Miss Blatch. 'She is very well now except for a little headache.'

The following evening the couple were in the ground-floor sitting room together when Miss Blatch told Mrs Lloyd that she had prepared a bath for her. The landlady then got on with her ironing. She later recalled:

> A few minutes after that I heard a sound from the bathroom. It was a sound of splashing. Then there was a noise as of someone putting wet hands or arms on the side of the bath, and then a sigh. The sigh was the last I heard. The next sound I heard was someone playing the organ in the sitting room.

It was a haunting tune – 'Nearer my God to Thee' – most famously played on the *Titanic* as it sank beneath the waves two years earlier. 'I should say the organ playing went on for about ten minutes,' said Miss Blatch. 'The next sound I heard was the front door slam.'

A few minutes later she heard the front doorbell and opened it to find Mr Lloyd holding a paper bag full of tomatoes.

'I forgot I had a key,' he told her, adding, 'I have been for some tomatoes for Mrs Lloyd's supper. Is she down yet?' He then went upstairs and called for his wife. A moment later, Miss Blatch heard him say, 'My God, there is no answer.'

'Perhaps she has gone to her bedroom,' replied Miss Blatch, helpfully.

As Mr Lloyd remembered it, he was anxious because his wife had not been well:

> I went from the ground floor to the first floor where the bathroom was. There was no light in the room, and I struck a match and lit the gas on the left-hand side going in. I then looked straight to the bath, and saw my wife under the water. The bath was about three parts full … When I lifted her up there was no sign of life, and all over her mouth was froth.

'When I got into the bathroom the prisoner had Mrs Lloyd in his arms,' Miss Blatch recalled. 'He was holding her up over the bath. Her legs were in the bath still. I felt her arm, and it was cold. I then said I would go for a doctor and a policeman.'

PC Stanley Heath was the first on the scene at around quarter past eight that evening. He found Mr Lloyd kneeling beside his wife 'working the arms of the woman backwards and forwards'. The officer then gave her mouth-to-mouth resuscitation until the doctor arrived to confirm that she was in fact dead. There was no sign of a struggle other than a small bruise on her left elbow, no evidence of poison, and no suggestion of a heart attack or brain haemorrhage. It was clear she had drowned.

Mr Lloyd's reaction to this sudden tragedy was to tell the doctor that he hoped the inquest would not return a verdict of suicide; 'as I should not like it said that my wife was insane.' Then when PC Heath informed him that the body would be removed 'in due course', he replied, 'Cannot it be removed tonight?' The next morning he set about arranging the funeral. He wanted the cheapest possible, and haggled the price down to £6 10s. On 23 December, Margaret Lloyd was buried in a common grave at Islington Cemetery.

The coroner's investigation came to the obvious conclusion that this was an accidental death. But they were unaware of several telling details that pointed suspiciously towards murder.

Six days before her sudden demise, Margaret Lloyd (then known by her maiden name of Margaret Lofty) had finalised an insurance policy that would pay out £700 in the event of her death. She had not told her family about it, or informed them of her plans to marry. The first her family knew of the wedding was in a letter Margaret sent on the evening of 16 December, shortly after arriving at Bismarck Road:

> No doubt you will be surprised to know that I was married today to a gentleman named John Lloyd. He is a thorough Christian man, who I have known since June. I met him at Bath … I have every proof of his love for me. He has been honourable and kept his word to me in everything. He is such a nice man …

The next day, a few hours before her death, she visited a solicitor's office at No. 84 Islington High Street and asked to draw up a will naming her husband as sole beneficiary. She was adamant it had to be typed out and signed straight away.

All of this was done at the request of her husband, John Lloyd. Except his name was not John Lloyd at all, it was George Joseph Smith, a forty-two-year-old serial bigamist and swindler with a taste for romantic poetry and passionate letters. He had first married in 1898 but since then had accrued seven other 'wives' with the aim of stealing all of their money. Two of these women, like Margaret Lofty, had drowned in the bath.

Smith's downfall began with an innocuous story in the *News of the World* headlined: 'Found Dead in Bath – Bride's Tragic Fate on Day after Wedding'. The report of Margaret Lloyd's death was spotted by Charles Burnham, whose daughter, Alice, had died at a boarding house in Blackpool on 12 December 1913, five weeks after marrying George Joseph Smith. She too had taken out life insurance. Her death was reported with the strikingly similar headline: 'Bride's Sudden Death in Bath'. Mr Burnham contacted his local police in Aylesbury and both newspaper clippings were sent to Scotland Yard. The case was taken up by Inspector Arthur Neil, who set about interviewing the landlady at No. 14 Bismarck Road as well as the local doctor, PC Heath and the undertaker. His suspicions that John Lloyd and George Joseph Smith were the same man were confirmed on 1 February 1915, when he and his officers cornered 'John Lloyd' in Shepherd's Bush. At first he denied being Smith, but when he realised that Mr Burnham would identify him, he confessed to using a false name on the register of his marriage to Margaret Lofty. 'But that is all you can put against me,' he added. 'You may think it strange, but it was the irony of fate that my two wives should have died in the same way.'

Two wives accidentally drowned in a bath may have been a coincidence, but three was beyond belief. Later that February, after it was reported that Alice Smith's body was being exhumed, Scotland Yard received information about the death of Bessie Mundy in a bath in Herne Bay. She had married a man named Henry Williams in Weymouth in August 1910, but he had disappeared with £100 of her money a month later. Then, in May 1912, she ran into him again and allowed herself to be duped a second time. In her eyes he was an art dealer, a popular gentleman, and 'a good and kind husband'. She made a will naming him as the beneficiary of her £2,500 estate and five days later he found her dead in the bathtub at their room in a boarding house in Herne Bay, Kent. Henry Williams was, of course, George Smith.

The police bolstered their circumstantial case with the evidence of the pathologist Bernard Spilsbury, who had already seen Dr Crippen and Frederick Seddon off to the gallows. Spilsbury's theory was that Smith drowned his victims by pulling up their feet as they lay in the bath, causing their heads to be submerged. The sudden rush of fluid into their nose and mouth would cause an immediate blackout, preventing them from struggling to raise their head above water. He recruited a young swimmer to test his hypothesis:

From the ankle I lifted up her legs very suddenly. She slipped under easily, but to me, who was closely watching, she seemed to make no movement. Suddenly I gripped her arm, it was limp. With a shout I tugged at her armpit and raised her head above the water. It fell over to one side. She was unconscious. For nearly half an hour my detectives and I worked away at her with artificial respiration and restoratives. Things began to look serious, and then a quick change began to take place, and her pretty face began to take on the natural bloom of young healthy womanhood … She told us afterwards that immediately she went under the water with her legs held in the air, the water just rushed into her mouth and up her nostrils. That was all she knew, as she remembered no more until she came to and saw all our anxious faces bending over.

On 22 June 1915, Smith was tried for the murder of Bessie Mundy at the Old Bailey. The case was supported with evidence of the deaths of both Alice Burnham and Margaret Lofty, but it was still circumstantial – nobody had ever caught George Joseph Smith in the act. Smith's lawyer, Edward Marshall Hall, argued that he was not the kind of man who could commit 'one of the most diabolical series of crimes that any records of any country have ever produced'. Marshall Hall told the jury, 'A man who could commit such crimes as are alleged in this case is not only a criminal, but a monster without parallel.'

Smith did not give evidence in his defence, but he could not restrain himself from shouting out halfway through the judge's summing up: 'You may as well hang me the way you are going on,' he exclaimed. 'You can go on forever – you cannot make me into a murderer; I have done no murder.' The jury were not convinced by his protestations and found him guilty after deliberating for just twenty-two minutes. He was hanged at Maidstone Gaol on Friday 13 August 1915. According to the executioner John Ellis, Smith's last words were 'I am innocent!'

One question still remains however: why did George Joseph Smith bring his third murder victim to London, and Highgate in particular? There was no explanation given at the trial. But because the death of Margaret Lofty happened in the capital, it was reported by the national newspapers and was seen 240 miles away in Blackpool and 60 miles away in Herne Bay. Had he remained anywhere else in the country his crimes might have gone undetected for many more years, and many more women might have become one of those known as the Brides in the Bath.

# The Godfather

1943

| | |
|---|---|
| *Suspect:* | *Otavio Handley aka Darby Sabini* |
| *Age:* | *55* |
| *Charge:* | *Racketeering & Accepting Stolen Goods* |
| *Sentence:* | *Three years in prison* |

On 11 July 1888, two months before Jack the Ripper began his campaign of murder and mutilation in the East End, a child was born in the slums of Clerkenwell. Son of an Italian father and an English mother, the baby's name was registered as Otavio Handley. But it was as Darby Sabini that he would establish himself as one of the most feared gangsters in London. His criminal empire was built not on the smuggling of drugs or alcohol but on the racecourses, where the rich and titled gambled away their wealth. In the 1920s, at the height of his powers, it was estimated that he was raking in between £20,000 and £30,000 a year, the equivalent of more than £1 million today. His fame is thought to have earned him a place in Graham Greene's book *Brighton Rock* as the model for the gangster Colleoni. So how did an immigrant's son work his way up to become the Godfather of London?

Sabini's story began in an overcrowded dwelling at No. 4 Little Bath Street, only a short distance from the Middlesex House of Correction. It is now a characterless stretch of Eyre Street Hill between Summers Street and Warner Street, but in the late nineteenth century it was populated by Italian immigrants trying to scrape a living as ice-cream sellers and organ grinders. The census records for 1881 and 1891 show that during this period there were as many as twenty people crammed into the one house – the families of asphalt workers,

*An Ice-cream seller in Little Italy, by John Thomson, from Victorian London Street Life (1877).*

painters and decorators, fish salesmen, 'shopmen' and locket-case makers. The turnover of tenants was high, and by 1890 the Sabini family appears to have moved down the road to No. 1.

On 13 July that year, two days after Octavio's second birthday, his father, Ottavio Sabini (also known as Octavio or Joseph), witnessed the murder of Ugo Milandi, a twenty-two-year-old Italian barber. Milandi had made a joke at the expense of his friend Marzielli Vialli, a twenty-four-year-old 'looking-glass frame maker' ('What do you want to do business with that man for?') at the Anglo-Italian club in Eyre Street Hill. Vialli didn't see the funny side and plunged a knife into Milandi's thigh, severing his femoral artery. Ottavio Sabini, who tried to help the victim, later told the Old Bailey, 'I asked him how he felt – he said he did not feel very well. He died about five minutes afterwards, before we got to the hospital.'

Four years later, Ottavio Sabini again found himself giving evidence at the Old Bailey, but this time as the victim. On 4 November 1894, he was stabbed in the shoulder by a sixty-year-old pimp in Eyre Street Hill. Sabini, who described himself as an ice-cream salesman, told the Old Bailey that Thomasso Casella 'wanted 2s from me to go with this girl, and I wanted 3s if I gave him the 2s, to be repaid in a day or two – he wanted to give me only two pence.' It was against this background of casual street violence in Little Italy that the young Darby Sabini grew up.

His mother, Eliza 'Elizabeth' Handley, had at least six children before she married his father at St Paul's Church in Clerkenwell on 14 December 1898. His father, now forty-two, described himself as a 'carman' or delivery driver living at No. 112 Central Street. Two years later, when the family was living at No. 29 Mount Pleasant, eleven-year-old Otavio was enrolled at Laystall Street School (now Christopher Hatton Primary School). He left on his fourteenth birthday to continue his education on the streets of Clerkenwell.

Darby Sabini would later claim that he joined the East Surrey militia at the age of eighteen, before taking up professional boxing under the name of Fred Handley in his early twenties. Other accounts suggest that he was making his name as a middleweight fighter from his teens, before graduating to ring-side security. It is claimed that he and his brothers led a gang of Italians in an attack on the rival 'Titanic' mob in Hoxton, known as the 'Battle of the Nile', in 1908. It was just one of a series of conflicts between competing criminal groups around London, including the Elephant Boys (of Elephant and Castle), the Brummagens, the Finsbury Boys and the King's Cross Boys. Budding gangster or not, when the 1911 census came around Sabini, aged twenty-two, was living at home with his mother, his younger brothers Joseph, George and Harry, his sister Mary, a servant and three lodgers at No. 12 Bowling Green Lane in Clerkenwell. His occupation was given as 'assisting in business' to his mother, a coal dealer. Two years later, on 21 December 1913, he described himself as a carman living at No. 4 St Helen Street when he married twenty-two-year-old Annie Potter at St Phillip's Church in Clerkenwell.

Darby Sabini's rise to power is said to have begun with the humiliation of the leader of the Elephant Boys, Thomas 'Monkey' Benneworth, at the Griffin pub in Saffron Hill in 1920. When Benneworth ripped the dress of the Italian barmaid, Darby broke his jaw with a single knockout punch. But by this time the real action was on the racecourses. Like other gangs, the Sabini gang (otherwise known as 'The Italian Mob', even though Sabini could not speak the language) extorted money out of bookmakers using the threat of violence and, if necessary, a slash of the razor. It was such a lucrative business that rival mobs inevitably clashed over the spoils, with pitched battles, split lips and spilt blood at race meetings across the country. Typically, Darby Sabini would later claim that he was only involved as a steward with the Bookmakers and Racecourses Protection Association and was actually trying to stop Birmingham gangsters from blackmailing the bookmakers operating in the south.

The Sabini gang, showing Enrico Cortesi seated centre, with Darbi Sabini behind his left shoulder, (wearing a cap) and Harry Sabini over his right shoulder. (Islington Local History Centre)

At the same time, the Sabinis were also involved in running gambling and drinking dens. Yet somehow, despite being well known to police, Darby always managed to avoid prison. In May 1920 he was accused of 'keeping a gaming house' and bound over to the sum of £20 on condition that he did not frequent any such establishments for twelve months. The following year he was fined £10 after being caught with a revolver without a certificate, whilst trying to escape from the Brummagen gang at Greenford Trotting Track in north-west London. Sabini was cleared of the charge of 'shooting with intent' on the grounds of self-defence. Four days after that incident, on 27 March 1921, he invited the Brummagen leader, Billy Kimber, to London to discuss a proposal – he would stay away from the Midlands if Kimber's group kept away from the South. The meeting at a flat at No. 70 Colliers Street ended with Kimber receiving a bullet in his side. The notorious villain Alf Solomon, who was allied to Sabini at the time, claimed that he had fired the shot accidentally and was subsequently acquitted of attempted murder.

Gang warfare erupted even closer to home in the autumn of 1922 when the Cortesi brothers, long-time allies of the Sabinis, started agitating for a greater share of the profits. A feud broke out, and Enrico Cortesi (known as Harry Frenchie) is said to have threatened to kill Darby Sabini, adding, 'What have you ever shared with us apart from trouble? The Sabinis are becoming too big for their boots. We are the ones who pushed you up and we are the ones who can pull you down.' The stage was set for a brutal confrontation.

Shortly after midnight on 20 November, Darby Sabini, then thirty-four, and his younger brother Harry, twenty-two, were talking at the bar of the Fratellanza club on the corner of Great Bath Street and Warner Street, Clerkenwell. The barmaid at the club, Louisa Doralli (according to some accounts the goddaughter of Darby Sabini), was about to close for the night when the Cortesi brothers arrived and asked for coffee. Augustus Cortesi, thirty-four, said to Darby, 'Come on, this is the time to fight' and pulled out a revolver. Miss Doralli managed to grab his hand as he pulled the trigger and the shot missed its target. Enrico Cortesi, thirty-nine, then pulled out a gun and aimed it at Harry Sabini. Miss Doralli later told the *Daily Express*:

I threw myself between them. I don't know why except that I thought the man would not shoot at a woman. Quick as a thought Sabini drew me aside and at that moment the shots were fired. One hit Sabini in the stomach. He creased up and fell at my feet. I raised his head to my knee and he pointed at the wound, where the blood was beginning to stain his clothing. I do not know what happened after that. My head reels when I try to think of it and I can still hear the two shots.

Harry Sabini was taken to the Royal Free Hospital in Gray's Inn Road and was at first not expected to recover. Meanwhile, the police rounded up the Cortesis and searched for the leader Enrico, described in the newspapers as waddling like Charlie Chaplin and being 'sharp featured, about five feet eight inches tall with sallow complexion, brown hair, grey eyes and a pronounced Roman nose'. Surprisingly, Darby Sabini agreed to give evidence against the Cortesi gang at the Old Bailey and told jurors how Alexander Tomaso, thirty-one, had bludgeoned him over the head with a bottle, smashing his false teeth. Tomaso had been

Louisa Doralli, said to be the goddaughter of Darby Sabini, who saved their lives at the Fratellanza club in Clerkenwell in 1923. The man in the inset picture is Harry Sabini. Photos printed in the Daily Mirror in November 1922. (Author)

a friend, he explained, but they had fallen out when Tomaso tried to lure him into the extortion racket, selling lists of horses to bookmakers for 5s each. 'They earn £3,000 or £4,000 a year selling them,' Sabini told the court, 'sometimes as much as £100 or £200 a day.'

In their defence, the Cortesis complained that Harry Sabini had fired an automatic pistol in the club and that the Sabinis had been involved in a dozen cases of stabbings and shootings without prosecution. The judge, Mr Justice

Augustus and Enrico Cortesi, pictured in the Daily Mirror. (Author)

Paul and George Cortesi, pictured in the Daily Mirror. (Author)

Darling, saw this as his opportunity to turn his summing up into a riff on the 'Montagues and Capulets' of Shakespeare's *Romeo and Juliet*, who were always quarrelling among themselves. He also remarked on the origin of the 'Sabini' name:

> When Rome was founded, there was a deficiency of women. The Latins invited the Sabines to a party, carried off all the women they fancied and married them. It is recorded that the Sabine women made excellent wives. Apparently the colony which now inhabits Clerkenwell is one of the results.

The jury acquitted Tomaso, Paul Cortesi, thirty-one, and George Cortesi, thirty-three, but convicted Augustus and Enrico of attempted murder. Mr Justice Darling sentenced them leniently to three years in prison, on the basis that the victims were not exactly of good character.

From this point, Darby Sabini began to withdraw from the front line and left the dirty work to Harry. He even attempted to sue the *Topical Times* for describing him as a member of one of the turf gangs. When he failed to appear at court the writ was dismissed, and he was pursued at the Bankruptcy Court for debts of £810. At this hearing, Darby again claimed that he was only paid around £8 a week as a steward with the Bookmakers and Racecourse Protection Society 'to put down ruffianism at race meetings.' It was suggested that he was 'the king of the Sabini gang' and earned £20,000 to £30,000 a year. 'No, I do not admit that,' Sabini replied. He was careful not to flash his wealth and is said to have continued to live in shabby housing and wear poor men's clothes.

After being declared bankrupt, Sabini and his wife left Clerkenwell for good and moved to Hove in Sussex, directing operations from afar. Even fifteen years later, at the height of the Second World War, the authorities still thought him dangerous enough to lock up under Defence Regulation 1B, on the grounds that he had Italian sympathies and 'is liable to lead internal insurrections against this country'. MI5 appear to have been suggesting that if Italy entered the war then 'Italian consuls and leaders of the fascio will employ Italians of the gangster or racketeer type for certain violence'. A police memo from June 1940 added: 'He is a gangster of the worst type with a heavy following in the Italian Colony of racecourse bullies. He is a man of very violent disposition.' Five months later Darby pleaded his case, telling the committee that he had tried to join the Home Guard but was rejected on medical grounds: 'I have not got Italian sympathies. I wish we could go and lick them. It will not be long before they run away. They are cowards.' His wife also insisted that he was heavily involved in charity work and was the life governor of sixteen London hospitals – 'The whole of his life has been spent in helping others.' Darby was eventually released on 15 April 1941. Two years later he was jailed for three years for receiving stolen goods. He died in 1950, aged sixty-two.

Case Thirteen

# Coronation Roses

1937

| | |
|---|---|
| *Suspect:* | *Frederick George Murphy* |
| *Age:* | *52* |
| *Charge:* | *Murder* |
| *Sentence:* | *Execution* |

The day after being crowned King, George VI and his queen consort, Elizabeth Bowes-Lyon, surprised their delirious subjects with an unexpected tour around London. The royal car set off from Buckingham Palace at half past two on 13 May 1937, and made its way through the West End towards Shaftesbury Avenue. Word quickly spread as the new monarch was sighted in Theobald's Road and Clerkenwell Road, and by startled market sellers in Leather Lane. Then it was across to Old Street before striking northwards up Bath Street and Shepherdess Walk into Islington. Turning left on to Essex Road, the car drove past Harding's Furniture at No. 22 Islington Green, before doubling back to Upper Street. By now the crowds were enormous. Shoppers, shopkeepers, workers and idle passers-by, enjoying the half-day holiday, rushed into the street to catch a glimpse of their King. The *Mirror* newspaper reported:

> Tens of thousands of wildly excited children had the greatest surprise of their lives yesterday when the king and queen made an unannounced circular tour through fourteen miles of north London streets ... Outside Islington Town Hall police officers had to jump on the running boards of the royal car while fifty other officers ran alongside for nearly a mile. Women rushed

from a block of flats in Upper-street and waved their hands wet with soapsuds as the car passed. They had been washing when news of the visit reached them …

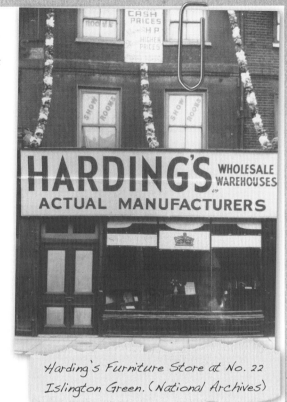

Harding's Furniture Store at No. 22 Islington Green. (National Archives)

The crowds lingered for a while before dissipating as the royal car completed its circular tour via Highbury, Offord Road, Caledonian Road, Kentish Town and Marylebone. The cheers and the smiles slowly faded as the men and women of Islington got back to work. King George VI and his queen returned to Buckingham Palace, blissfully unaware that they had passed the scene of a murder committed just hours earlier on Coronation Day itself. The victim's body was still lying in the cellar beneath Harding's Furniture Store when the royal car rolled through Islington Green and would not be discovered until the morning of the following day.

At around ten o'clock on 14 May 1937, the sales manager at Harding's, Stanley Wilton, was handed a message scrawled upon a piece of paper. It appeared to have come from the caretaker, Frederick George Murphy:

Dear Stan don't get frighten there is a dead woman in no 22 and you can believed me Stan it nothing to do with me but you know what the police will say it was me for sure but if they take the trouble to find out where I was all the time what they won't take the Trouble to do, Stan I can't write I to upset about it. Stan you can believed me I don't know anything about how this woman got in the cellar of no 22.

A perturbed Stanley Wilton and the manager, Godfrey Pollock, made a quick search of the shop before heading downstairs to the basement. It was dusty and dirty and full of bed frames and mattresses. At the far end, beneath the pavement outside the shop, the stone-floored cellar was so dark they had to light a candle. 'We found a lady's shoe in a corner there,' said Mr Wilton. 'A trunk was in the entrance of the coal cellar. Some brown paper was beyond the trunk. I lifted it and saw the hand of a female. I lifted the paper further and saw the profile and hair of a woman.' He then sent for the police.

The body was found in the cellar, behind the case, covered with brown paper. (National Archives)

Detective Inspector Arthur Lount noted that there was no sign that the dead woman had been dragged through the dirt into the coal cellar. Her stockings were still on, although her skirt had been drawn up slightly. She had been dead at least twenty-four hours. Blood trickled from the mouth and nose, and there was obvious bruising under the chin, suggesting strangulation. It was one of the easier cases of Dr Bernard Spilsbury's career. Bruising to the larynx, along the lower jaw and to the lips and tongue, together with a fracture of the hyoid bone in the neck, revealed death was caused by manual strangulation.

Later that night, the victim was identified as Rosina Field by her sister Mary Leat. Rosina was forty-nine years old, 5ft ¼in, with greying, dark brown hair. She was the mother of a grown-up daughter, Ivy Crafter, and was living apart from her husband at a hostel for women

Rosina Field, a forty-nine-year-old prostitute living at No. 13 Duncan Terrace in Islington. (National Archives)

at No. 13 Duncan Terrace. Although her sister was unaware of any 'habit of associating with men', Rosina appears to have earned her living as a prostitute. She was last seen alive leaving the hostel at seven o'clock on Coronation Day, wearing a dark blue coat with fur across the shoulder, a bright blue woollen jumper underneath, and a little hat.

The first person the police wanted to speak to was Frederick George Murphy, the author of the strange note about the body. He wasn't at his flat at No. 57a Colebrooke Row, but his partner Ethel Marshall knew about the dead body already – he had taken her down to the cellar to see it. According to Ethel they had been out drinking on 13 May and he had told her: 'I have got something serious to tell you. There's a woman's body in the shop.' She hadn't believed him and he had proved it by leading her down into the basement at Harding's. 'He was not upset … he said he was innocent and knew nothing whatever about it,' she told police. 'He said he found it there in the morning.'

Murphy was fifty-two years old, a thickset, unattractive hulk of a man with a mobster's face. He claimed to have been born in the East End and spent his early working life on ships travelling across the world. In Australia, he received a 'cut-throat scar' on his neck during a fight. Later he earned his way as a greengrocer, a coalman and an unsuccessful gambler at dog tracks. In between, he served short spells in prison for frequenting (a brothel most likely) in 1907, assault and living on prostitution in 1909, for vagrancy in 1913, theft in 1924 and attempted burglary in 1925. He called himself different names at different times – James Johnson, George Taylor, or just 'Mick'. His abiding passion, aside from betting on the dogs, was women, or more particularly prostitutes. Murphy had a history of offering women money for sex, including two other residents of the hostel at No. 13 Duncan Terrace. Edith Williams, sixty-four, declined the offer of 1s but Emily Robinson, a fifty-six-year-old charwoman, agreed to sex on a pile of mattresses in the corner of the dirty basement at Harding's in return for 8d. A porter had seen him taking Rosina Field into the shop a few months earlier, and a builder swore he had seen the two of them there on the morning of the Coronation at around six o'clock.

The police didn't have long to wait to get their hands on Murphy. In the early hours of 15 May he walked into the station at Poplar and asked to make a statement 'about the Islington murder'. His story was an unlikely one and involved taking a prostitute he knew as Rose (not Rosina Field) into Harding's for 'sexual intercourse standing up in the passage way', on Coronation Day evening. As they left, he had given her 2s 6d and then went to put some money on a dog race and to have a drink at the pub with his 'missus' Ethel Marshall. The next morning, the 13th, he went to the shop to sweep up. 'I put the light on and saw a woman lying on the floor near some mattresses,' he said in his statement. 'She was lying longways in the basement … her head towards the cellar door.' Murphy said he waited for the manager to arrive but when that didn't happen he went back to the basement, picked up the body and carried it into the cellar. He covered her with the fur coat, put the brown paper over that and then moved the tin trunk in front of the body, 'so nobody could see it and get frightened.'

Murphy claimed that after writing the note for Mr Wilton he decided to commit suicide. 'I went to Stratford, hung around there walking up and down the canal bank. At about 11 p.m. I did try to hang myself by the railway bridge.' His makeshift noose snapped and he ended up in a heap, still very much alive, on the ground. 'I then made up my mind to go to the police and tell them what I knew about the dead woman.' His defence to the charge of murder was, in the words of Murphy himself, 'I didn't do her in but I admit I handled the body.'

The police believed that the 'Rose' he admitted meeting on Coronation night was Frances Keen, who lived with Rosina Field at No. 13 Duncan Terrace. She told detectives that she went drinking with him in the Carved Red Lion on the corner of St Peter's Street and Essex Road. On several occasions he had asked her back

Photo of No. 13 Duncan Terrace today. (Author)

to the shop but she had always refused. The next night, at the same pub, he told her about the body – 'Well Rose don't be frightened if I tell you,' he said. 'When I went on Coronation night I saw a body lying on the floor. For Christ's sake Rose, don't tell anybody else.'

Murphy's cack-handed attempt to explain away the woman he had been seen taking into Harding's on Coronation night was further demolished by the evidence of Herbert Fennings, a car-park attendant for Collins' Music Hall across the road. Mr Fennings, who knew both Murphy and Rosina by sight, had seen them meet up in Islington Green at around eight o'clock that night. 'They went down past Collins' towards the furniture shop,' he said. 'That was the last time I saw the woman.' Murphy was seen at the Queen's Head pub at half nine and at the Fox at ten o'clock. Later that night he was seen by Mr Fennings walking with his partner Ethel Marshall. If he had killed Rosina Field, it must have been between eight and half nine that night.

Murphy's defence didn't convince the jury at the Old Bailey either. On 2 July 1937, he was convicted of murder. Like Frederick Seddon, he saw his last words as a chance to criticise the case against him and to proclaim his innocence to the judge, the Lord Chief Justice. 'In your summing up my Lord you did not give one good word for me. You told the jury I was nothing else but a liar, that I was telling nothing but lies.'

The judge responded, 'You know as well as I know that the verdict is right,' and pronounced the death sentence with the traditional ending: 'May God have mercy on your soul.'

Murphy sneered, 'Mercy on my soul – oh, yes!', as he was taken down to the cells. He would spend the next six weeks at Pentonville Prison awaiting execution. The *News of the World* said he would:

Go down in history as the most callous prisoner who has ever occupied the condemned cell ... he plays cards and draughts all day long and at night enjoys a glass of beer with which he toasts his guardians, the judges who tried him and the detectives who brought about his conviction.

Murphy was quoted as saying, 'I will meet whatever waits me smiling.'

The end came at nine o'clock on the morning of 17 August 1937. But Frederick George Murphy still had one last card to play, even after death. Five days later, the *News of the World* printed Murphy's stunning confession to another murder. And by a strange, sinister twist of fate, this earlier victim was also known as 'Rose'.

At around twenty-five to one on the morning of 12 March 1929, Inspector Sidney Jordan of M Division was on patrol with a sergeant in Elstead Street in Walworth, south London. At the end of a block of flats known as Hearns buildings he spied what looked like a bundle of clothes lying in the street. 'We found it was a woman, lying on her back, still,' he recalled. 'Her head was on the roadway, her feet on the footpath. She was breathing very stentoriously. I saw blood on the road under the woman's head. We opened her coat and found she was bleeding from a wound in her throat.' Within fifteen minutes the woman was dead – in all likelihood the officers had only missed catching the killer red-handed by a few moments.

The victim was forty-five-year-old Katherine Peck, who lived with her husband and nineteen-year-old son in Flint Street, Walworth. In recent years, for whatever reason, she had started staying out late at night to work on the streets and was known by her friends as 'Singing Rose' or 'Rose Sullivan'. She had started hanging around with a man variously known as Tim Murphy or Tubby Murphy, a man who wasn't afraid to punch her in the face if he saw her chatting to other men. This same Murphy was with her when she was last seen alive, at around ten o'clock on 11 March, outside a pub in Mansell Street near Aldgate. Three hours later Murphy returned to his 8d a night bed at a lodging house in Tooley Street, alone.

Murphy gave several different explanations as to his movements that night. He told one friend that he had left her 'safe and sound at 11.15 p.m.'. When interviewed by police, he claimed that he walked with her from Gardner's Corner across the river to the junction of Tower Bridge Road and Grange Road before heading back to his lodgings at around midnight. The nearest he got to the truth was what he told one of his friends at Aldgate the following afternoon. 'I've done the old woman in,' he explained. 'I'm on the run.' He remained at large for another two weeks, before handing himself in at Bethnal Green police station.

Despite the confession, the lack of an alibi, and the fact he was the last to be seen with the victim, detectives were unable to pin down his movements between half ten and the finding of the body two hours later. His trial, which began on 28 May 1929, ended in his acquittal. It was another eight years until the police's suspicions were confirmed by Murphy's confession. He had written it shortly after walking free from court, safe in the knowledge that he could not be charged twice with the same crime. It remained locked away in a safe for eight years before being handed over to the *News of the World* after his death.

In his tortuous scrawl, Murphy claimed that he had armed himself with a 'chive' or tobacco knife in anger when Katherine Peck had refused to leave the pub and laughed in his face.

> I got hold of her and pulled her out. When we got near her home she asked me for fourpence. There was a quarrel. She tried to take a lump out of me. I gave her a dig with my chive … and I left her. She was lying on the ground … that's the whole story. The rest you know. I now want to leave England forever.

Sadly for Rosina Field, he did not leave England. Instead of counting himself a lucky man, he pestered the police with a series of letters accusing the police and the key witness of perjury. He openly vowed that he would one day hang for killing a police officer and boasted that he had procured a gun to take revenge on those who had tried to convict him of the murder of Katherine Peck. Murphy, claimed the *News of the World*, was 'the vainest, toughest and most callous of murderers'.

# Notes and Sources

**Stand and Deliver!**: The main source for the life of Claude Duval is 'The Memoirs of Monsieur Du Vall', containing the history of his life and death (1670), printed in Thomas Osborne's *Harleian Miscellany, Vol. 3*, pp.295–299. The 'faithfully recorded' version by Edwin T. Woodhall, *Claude Duval, Gentleman Highwayman and Knight of the Road*, was printed in 1937. One of the few mentions of Duval in action was apparently made in a newsletter in 1666 after a highwayman politely asked a group of gentlemen for their money so he could bet it on a horse called 'Boopeepe' at Newmarket. 'It is thought that it was Monsieur Claud Du Vall, or one of his knot.'

**Dick Turpin**: Contemporary reports of Dick Turpin in Islington can be found in *The London Magazine*, Sunday 22 May 1737; *Daily Gazetteer*, 24 May 1737; *Weekly Miscellany*, 27 May 1737. He may have been given credit for robberies that he was not involved in – see the *London Evening Post* of 7 June 1737, which reported: 'Last Tuesday morning, about ten o'clock, three gentlemen coming from Highgate in Mr Dacosta's Coach were robb'd of about 17l [£17]. By a single Highwayman, whom they suppos'd to be the famous Turpin.'

Newspaper reports of his crimes all over London were collected in a book by Arty Ash and Julius Day, *Immortal Turpin: The Authentic History of England's most Notorious Highwayman* (1948). See also James Sharpe, *Dick Turpin: The Myth of the English Highwayman* (2005), Christopher Hibbert, *Highwaymen* (1967), John Nelson, *The History and Antiquities of the Parish of Islington* (1829), and the fictional versions of Turpin's life in William Harrison Ainsworth's *Rookwood* (1834) and Henry Downes Miles' *The Life of Richard Palmer; Better Known as Dick Turpin, the Notorious Highwayman and Robber* (1839).

**The Thief-taker:** See the Proceedings of the Old Bailey online for details on the trials of Jack (Joseph) Sheppard (t17240812-52), John Wigley (t17210830-51), James Reading (t17210830-50) and William Burridge (t17220228-30). Further details on Wild can be found in Gerald Howson's *Thief-Taker General, the Rise and Fall of Jonathan Wild* (1970); and on the Fielding brothers in *The Life and Work of Sir John Fielding* by R. Leslie Melville; newspaper reports on houses in West Street in *Illustrated London News*, 17 August 1844; *Morning Post*, 7 August 1844; *Lloyd's Weekly*, 11 and 18 August 1844; the *Examiner*, 17 and 18 August 1844. See also Spinks, *History of Clerkenwell*, and *Old and New London, Vol. 3*.

**A Duel:** The famous seventeenth-century scientist Robert Boyle examined the waters of Sadler's Wells in 1684 for *his Short Memoirs for the Natural Experimental History of Mineral Waters*. There are various accounts of Sadler's Wells and Musick House in Pinks' *History of Clerkenwell*, Thornbury's *Old and New London* and Nelson's *History of Islington*. See also *A True and Exact Account of Sadler's Well*, published by T.G. Doctor of Physick (1684) and *The Story of Sadler's Wells 1683 to 1964* by Dennis Arundel. Trial of Patrick French for murder in Proceedings of the Old Bailey, t17120910-28.

**The Cricket Field:** The description of White Conduit House in *Old and New London* and Spinks, *History of Clerkenwell*. In 1784 it was reported that a cricket match was played in the fields by the Duke of Forset, Lord Winchelsea, Lord Talbot, and other dignitaries. The field was apparently abandoned by the club for Marylebone because Islington was 'too public'. For the Fryer case see Martin Clinch and John Mackley in *The New and Complete Newgate Calendar* by William Jackson, p.491, and the Proceedings of the Old Bailey online, t17970531-1.

**Clowns and Robbers:** The original resting place of Joseph Grimaldi and his mentor Charles Dibdin are marked by a clever piece of public art in the same garden area, near to Pentonville Road. Phosphor bronze tiles have been set into the ground in the shape of two coffins, which when danced upon play musical notes. Grimaldi's 'casket' is tuned so that you can play his most famous song 'Hot Codlins'. The story of the Pentonville Robbers is told in the *Memoirs of Joseph Grimaldi* by Charles Dickens. See also Richard Findlater's *Grimaldi, King of Clowns* (1955), and Andrew McConnell Scott's *The Pantomime Life of Joseph Grimaldi* (2009).

**House of Blood**: Accounts of the murders, the inquest and the burials in *The Times*, 10, 11, 12 and 17 September 1834; *Morning Chronicle*, 11 September 1834; *Royal Gazette*, 25 November 1834; agency copy in the *Sydney Herald*, 29 January 1835; Edmund Burke's *Annual Register of World Events* for 1834; Reports of the 'museum' in Pinks, *History of Clerkenwell*, pp.507–510; and the *Standard*, 3 October 1834.

**Who Killed Mr Templeman?**: Charles Dickens would refer to the Templeman case in a letter to the Home Secretary on 3 July 1840, a few days before Gould left for Australia. Dickens wrote that:

> The terrors of transportation and confinement under the present system are known to few but those who have penetrated to the heart of parliamentary reports and commissioners' enquiries; by that class for whose especial benefit and correction they are intended, they are known least of all. I have felt this for a long time, and have had my old thoughts upon the subject wakened up afresh by the sentence passed upon the convict Gould the other day, which is shorn of its impressiveness and example by the one unfortunate circumstance that the people do not know, and do not suspect, what his real punishment is ... It has occurred to me that a strong and vivid description of the terrors of Norfolk Island and such-like places, told in a homely Narrative with a great appearance of truth and reality and circulated in some very cheap and easy form (if with the direct authority of the Government, so much the better) would have a very powerful impression on the minds of the badly disposed and ... would have a deep and salutary effect in inspiring all rising convicts with a tremendous fear of the higher penalties of the law ... I would have it on the pillow of every prisoner in England.

Dickens' plan never became reality. It is not known what happened to Richard Gould after his arrival in Australia on the ship *Eden*. There was however a twist in the tale as regards to the Templeman family. In 1873, John Templeman's great grandson, Herbert Templeman, a forty-two-year-old clerk at his father's firm of solicitors, was charged with forgery in relation to a £1,242 fraud on a Major General Morris of Tiverton. He was convicted at the Old Bailey the following year and sentenced to fifteen years' penal servitude. See Proceedings of the Old Bailey, reference t18740202-179.

The account of the Templeman murder is taken from reports in *The Times*, *Standard*, *Morning Post*, *Morning Chronicle* and the *Examiner* between March and June 1840. Both trials can be found on the Proceedings of the Old Bailey website. See also the file on the Templeman murder at the National Archives under reference MEPO 3/43.

**No. 39 Hilldrop Crescent**: Details of the Crippen case are taken from the Proceedings of the Old Bailey online; *Supper with the Crippens* by David James Smith; *Crippen the Mild Murderer* by Tom Cullen; and *Dr Crippen* by Katherine Watson. See also reports in the *Mirror*, 16 July 1910; *Islington Daily Gazette*, 15 July, 20 September and 12 October 1910. References to Belle Elmore in *The Stage* newspaper between 1907 and 1910. Details on the exploits of Sandy McNab in the *Western Times*, 21 September 1910, and 2 April 1912; *The Stage* newspaper between 1907 and 1914; and the *Mirror*, 25 June 1914.

**No. 63 Tollington Park**: Details of the Seddon case are taken from the Proceedings of the Old Bailey online; *Trial of the Seddons*, ed. Filson Young (1925); and *The Trial of the Seddons* by Edgar Wallace (1966).

**No. 14 Bismarck Road**: Reports on the changing of Bismarck Road to Waterlow Road in the *Derby Daily Telegraph*, 16 June 1916, and *The Times*, 26 January and 27 November 1916. A transcript of the trial can be found in *Notable British Trials: The Case of George Joseph Smith*, ed. Eric R. Watson. See also George Sims, *The Bluebeard of the Bath* (1915); Arthur La Bern, *The Life and Death of a Ladykiller* (1967); and Jane Robins, *The Magnificent Spilsbury and the Case of the Brides in the Bath* (2010).

**The Godfather**: Sabini appears to have given his date of birth as both 9 July 1888 and 9 July 1889. The only registered birth that comes close to a match is that of Otavio Handley, born to Charles Handley and Elizabeth Eliza Handley, *née* Fryer, at No. 4 Little Bath Street on 11 July 1888. Eliza Handley, who had a brother called Charles Handley, appears to have adopted the Sabini surname by 1891, when she is shown as living at No. 52 Warner Street with Joseph Sabini, aged thirty-six, and three sons: Frederick, aged ten, Charles, aged eight, and Thomas, aged three, and a five-month-old daughter called Mary. Eliza Handley, daughter of William Handley, married Ottavio Sabini, the son of farmer Regenti Sabini, at St Paul's Church, Clerkenwell, in 1898. There was another Otavio Sabini born on 7 August 1889, at No. 4 Back Hill, Clerkenwell, to Guiseppe and Domenica Sabini, but he died a year and sixteen days later of bronchitis. See also Brian McDonald, *Gangs of London* (2010); Edward T. Hart, *Britain's Godfather* (1993); and James Morton, *East End Gangland* (2009). Reports of cases involving the elder Sabini can be found in the online Proceedings of the Old Bailey, references t18941119-32 and t18900908-669. An Ottavio Sabini was also acquitted of wounding at a trial at the Clerkenwell Sessions on 3 September 1888. Darby Sabini's own brief version of his early years is recorded in a Home Office memo found in the National Archives, in the file HO 45/23691. These papers also contain details of his criminal record and his detention during the Second World War as a potential enemy of the state. Details of the fight at the Fratellanza are also taken from reports in *The Times*, the *Mirror* and the *Daily Express* from 21 November 1922, and 16–19 January 1923. Report of bankruptcy proceeding in *Daily Express*, 30 June 1926.

**Coronation Roses**: Description of Coronation crowds in *Mirror* and *The Times*, 14 May 1937. Rosina Field and Katherine Peck case details from witness statements and documents kept at National Archives CRIM 1/940; MEPO 3/874; HO 144/20658; CRIM 1/465. Murphy's confession in the *News of the World*, 22 August 1937.